HELLO
MY NAME IS

REDISCOVERING AMAZING STORIES OF THE OLD TESTAMENT

Shekinah
Reflections
PUBLICATIONS

Shekinah Reflection Publishing

ISBN-13: 978-1548875732
ISBN-10: 1548875732

The author can be contacted at ShekinahReflection@gmail.com

Dedicated to

My Church Family
in Saskatoon

CONTENTS

Welcome to the Party

Imagine attending a party with a huge guest list. The room is filled with people. Some you know very well; they have been your close friends for years. Some you know at an acquaintance level; you have met on occasion but you don't really keep in touch. Some you don't know at all; you couldn't pick them out of a line up if they were the only one in it. There you are mingling around in a large room, chit-chatting and sipping punch.

Things are going tolerably well for you as you stay close to those with whom you are familiar, but then it happens: someone walks up to you, extends their hand and says "Hi!" Immediately your nerves are kicked into gear. The face is vaguely familiar, but the name just isn't coming to you. You feel like you should know *something* about them, but your mind is drawing a complete blank. As you grab this pseudo-stranger's outstretched hand you realize there is only one thing that is going to save you from this impending faux pas and social disaster. Luckily for you, the wise person who put this little shindig together had the foresight to require all guests to wear those infamous "Hello, My Name is..." badges. You subtly adjust your position and attempt to discretely glance at the stranger's left lapel. Your eyes find their mark just as hands clasp and you enthusiastically cheer, "DAVE! So good to see you! How have you been?"

We've all been there, right? Trying desperately to make meaningful conversation with someone we are supposed to know, but frankly, can't remember much more than some of the most basic facts about – and we're not even 100 percent sure we've got those all exactly right. It happens when we cross paths with someone we used to know, but haven't seen much lately. Someone we used to be close to, but we've lost touch. Someone who epitomized the difference between a social network 'friend' and an actual real-life friend. The face is vaguely familiar. The name rings a bell. There are a few sketchy details that come to mind, but they are significantly outnumbered by the blanks left to fill.

I think Bible stories end up that way for many of us. Stories we heard week after week in Sunday school, characters we used to be incredibly familiar with have slipped away to the cobwebby corners of our minds. Story details get fuzzy. Character traits and personalities fade. Every now and then a name comes up and we think to ourselves, "Oh yeah, I know that guy." However, if we were ever pressed to say exactly what we knew about that guy, it may not be very much at all. Perhaps you've heard the phrase, "The devil is in the details." Well, when it comes to great stories, the drama is in the details and therefore when the details of a story get lost, so does much of the story's drama.

It is so easy for us, as adults, to lose the awe and wonder, the shock and surprise, the *oooh* and *aaaah* that some of the great stories of the Bible hold. It's so easy for these stories to lose their well-deserved wow factor by a lethal combination of being over-told and under-remembered.

The goal of this book is to retell these fantastic stories in a new and fresh way. To make the characters come alive and jump off the page. To put the reader right in the middle of the action. To remind us of the amazing things that happen in these stories, but even more importantly reacquaint us with the amazing God who was behind them. To be the name tag sticker that jogs our memory and prompts us to say, "Oh yeah. I remember you. Good to see you again!"

Hello, My Name is

HELLO
MY NAME IS
Pharaoh

You Shall Not Pass

Hello, my name is Pharaoh. I'm sure you've heard of me. I'm a pretty big deal. I was the divine ruler of the great empire of Egypt - the most powerful man in the whole world. My country was prosperous, my army was strong, my territory was vast and my ego was enormous.

I inherited the throne from my father, but I also inherited the empire's most annoying problem: the Hebrews. The Hebrews were an uncivilized band of nomads who had somehow snuck into Egypt centuries ago and had since become a serious pain in the neck. They were uncultured, they did not worship Ra or the other Egyptian gods and they all stunk like sheep. They claimed that at one point their ancestor, Joseph I believe they called him, was the top official in the land, second to only the king himself. Of course, that was completely laughable. There's no way in Duat that any Egyptian king would ever make someone like a Hebrew a low-level official let alone the top ruler in the land. I'm sure that was just some old folk story they invented to make themselves feel better than the peasant workers they really were.

For a long time, the Hebrews were just an annoyance. Sure, they were dirty and smelly, but we kept them on the outskirts of polite society and had them do all the unpleasant and nasty jobs respectable Egyptians didn't want to get their hands dirty doing. The only problem was their numbers were growing rapidly. At first, that wasn't cause for concern, but then we began to realize that, if war ever broke out and the Hebrews sided with our enemies, we could be in serious trouble – not because they possessed any special skills, but based on the sheer numbers alone. So, my ancestors made the Hebrews our slaves. The king's men worked these foreigners hard and punished them harshly whenever they got out of line. It's not that we were bad guys, it was just important that the Hebrews learned their rightful place in the grand scheme of things.

Perplexingly, the slaves continued to prosper and multiply, even under the most unfavorable circumstances. Eventually, my grandfather was forced to take more severe measures. He decreed that whenever a male Hebrew baby was born it should be immediately thrown into the mighty Nile River. This plan should have ensured that the Hebrew population would start to dwindle back to more manageable numbers. But somehow that didn't happen.

The upside of having so many of them around was it gave me plenty of laborers to build great cities and monuments in my own honor. The downside was they still posed a security risk and they weren't always entirely cooperative. Nonetheless, my slave drivers were sadistically hard on their Hebrew workers which seemed, for the most part, to keep them in line. That is until *he* showed up.

He said his name was Moses and that God had sent him. I asked him which one. He said, "*The* God," which made no sense to me at the time, so I just assumed he was talking about some god the Hebrews had made up to fabricate some sense of hope in their otherwise dismal existence.

At first, I didn't know what to make of this Moses guy. He claimed to have grown up in the courts of the Pharaoh. I found that hard to believe. I remember my father telling me stories about some kid his aunt had fished out of the river and raised as her own, but he lost it and went AWOL 40 years ago or more. He certainly didn't look like an Egyptian. He was dressed like a Midianite, but claimed to be a Hebrew. My first thought was perhaps the slaves had negotiated some kind of deal with the kings of Midian and this was a covert attempt to weaken my empire and leave it vulnerable to attack.

"The God says, 'let my people go!'" Moses demanded.

"You've got to be joking," I scoffed. "The Hebrews are my slaves and they ain't going nowhere, except back to work!"

I was determined to put a quick and permanent end to it all before this Moses character could rally any support around him. So, I sent out word to all my commanders declaring, "The required daily quota will not change, but inform the Hebrews that they will now be required to gather their own straw to use in the bricks they make. If they do not meet their daily quota, beat the foreman severely. If the people ask why this hardship has come upon them, tell them it is all because of this troublemaker, Moses."

And that's exactly what my men did. It seemed to be working well at first, but then, somehow, Moses managed to turn the Hebrews hearts against me. Several days later the old man was back in front of me again. This time he brought along his even older brother, Aaron.

"The God says, 'let my people go'," Moses repeated. "And just to let you know what you're dealing with, check this out."

Aaron threw his staff onto the floor and it transformed into a snake. It was a very cool trick, but one I had seen before. I called for my personal magicians. They were really good! Each of them threw their staff on the ground which then turned into snakes as well. However, my moment of smugness was short lived as Aaron's snake slithered around and quickly devoured all the other serpents. I'll admit, that was somewhat unnerving, but I wasn't about to change my mind.

The next morning, I went down to the Nile to bathe and Moses was there waiting for me. He repeated his request to have the Hebrews released and when I refused Moses gave his brother a nod. Aaron held his staff over the water and the entire river turned to blood. The stench was horrible and all the fish began floating belly-up in the river. I returned to the palace and found even the water stored in buckets and jars had turned. I ordered wells be dug on the shores of the Nile so fresh water could be collected. I called my magicians again and watched as they caused a basin of this fresh water to turn red as well. Of course, it wasn't the same as turning the whole river, but it was good enough for me because I was determined to not be swayed by anything Moses said or did, no matter what.

The troublemaker showed up again a week later, singing the same old tune: let my people go. Of course, I said no. Then Aaron waved his magic stick and frogs started flooding out of every river, stream, and canal in the land. My magicians tried to replicate this trick as well. I'm not sure if it worked or not, but the frogs kept coming. What they couldn't do is make it stop, so I told Moses to do it. However, to rule out coincidence I told him exactly when it should happen. Sure enough, the next morning, just as I had requested, all the frogs died. The only problem was now there were frogs everywhere, and I mean everywhere. We tried to clean things up but there were heaps of dead frogs rotting in the street and reeking to high Aaru. I had promised Moses that, if he stopped the frogs, I would let the Hebrews leave, temporarily, but now that the problem had been solved, I changed my mind.

Shortly thereafter, Moses returned. Aaron hit the ground with his staff and suddenly swarms and swarms of gnats were everywhere. It was miserable. I told my magicians to do this trick too, but they failed me. They even had the nerve to suggest the God must be doing it, but I assumed that was just an excuse. Moses returned again with the same old plea.

When I refused, the entire kingdom was overcome with flies. It was absolutely miserable, so I finally caved and told Moses the Hebrews could leave just long enough to have a festival to worship their god. But they could not go far or be gone for long. He agreed and when I woke up the next morning there was not a fly to be found anywhere.

Now that the pressure was off, I reconsidered and rescinded my previously granted permission. This irritated Moses, so when he returned, and I denied his request, he told me all of the livestock in the land – the horses, donkeys, camels, cattle, sheep, and goats – would die. Sure enough, that's exactly what happened, well, almost exactly. By some fluke, all of the livestock owned by the Israelites were fine.

Next, Moses made festering boils appear on every Egyptian in the land. They were so excruciatingly painful that when I called for my magicians, they could not even make it to the palace. Then, Moses predicted a severe hail storm would come – the worst we had ever seen. Some of my people had been swayed by this menace of a man and they made sure all their livestock and servants and everything of value was kept inside. I urged people to not be suckered in and stand in defiance of this rabble-rouser. Sure enough, the next day hail rained down from the sky, like rocks from a slingshot, decimating everything not safely under cover. I begged

Moses to make it stop, swearing I would let the Hebrews leave. He did; I didn't.

Moses returned, yet again, clearly ticked off at my numerous broken promises. His next curse brought locusts to Egypt. There were so many they literally covered the entire ground. They ate every plant, fruit, and leaf that had survived the hail. Again, I promised to let the Hebrews go if the plague was taken away. This time I meant it. However, once the pests were gone I came to my senses and refused.

"What do I have to do to make you see the light?" Moses said sounding quite exasperated. "How about this? For the next three days, the sun will be blotted out and the land of Egypt will be in complete and utter darkness."

This time this brigand had gone too far. Ra was the greatest of all Egyptian gods and I knew that Ra, and only Ra, controlled the sun. The old man could bluster all he wanted, but the sun wasn't going anywhere.

I confidently declared, "Won't happen." It did. To end the darkness, I negotiated a deal with Moses that permitted the Hebrews to leave the region temporarily to worship their god and allowed them to take their wives, children, livestock and other possessions with them. I knew this would increase the odds that they might try to make a run for it, but I was desperate. Besides, I had a huge military and could easily bring them back by force if need be. Moses agreed and the light returned. So did my resolve, and I recanted the deal once again.

Moses returned and spoke solemnly. "This is the last time I'm going to ask, please, let my people go." I refused. "I would not wish this upon my worst enemy, but if you do not reconsider, tonight every first-born child in the land of Egypt will die. Not one household will be spared; however, not a single Hebrew family will suffer this horrific fate."

He was bluffing, surely. The previous tricks were impressive, but this time he had overplayed his hand. He was obviously getting desperate. I was wrong. So very, very wrong. That night there was wailing all over the land as what Moses had predicted came to pass. I summoned Moses in the middle of the night and shouted, "Get out! All of you! Get out now!"

The Hebrews were all packed and ready to go. Their neighbors had given them gold, silver, and clothing as gifts, for the people were all in awe of the power of the God. So, Moses led his people out of Egypt with all of their families, livestock, and possessions. They even took with them the bones of their ancestor, Joseph.

It wasn't long before my grief turned to anger. It was clear the Hebrews had no intention of coming back, so I gathered my six hundred best chariots, along with every other chariot, horseman, and soldier I could find or conscript and set out to chase them down and bring them back. We caught up to them on the shores of the Red Sea. I was elated when I realized they were trapped. There was no way out. No escape. I would reclaim my slave labor workforce and, once we were back in Egypt I would make them sorely regret everything they had done. My punishment would be so harsh they would not even remotely consider such a foolhardy endeavor again.

As I was about to send my men in to round them up, a dense cloud floated in and hid the Hebrews from my sight. Eventually, the cloud drifted across the sea and what I saw shocked me. The waters had miraculously been divided, and a wide path of dry ground led to the other side. Almost all of the Hebrews already stood on the far shore. I had no idea how the trickster had pulled it off, but it really didn't matter. Nothing was going to stop me from getting my revenge and getting my slaves back.

I sounded the advance and my entire army raced across the dry seabed toward the far shore. We were about halfway across when the wheels began to fall off. Literally. Chariots, horses, and men all began to get stuck in the muddy ground. Many of my men tried to flee, believing that the God was fighting for the Hebrews. I looked across and gazed at Moses with an icy-and-hate-filled stare. The last thing I saw was Moses waving his hand over the seashore. There was a deafening rumble, and I was instantly swallowed up by the warm waters. The weight of my impressive armor made it impossible for me to swim to the surface. I perished that day, at the bottom of the sea along with my entire army.

When Moses first showed up in my throne room and told me the God was going to free His people and lead them out of Egypt to a land He had promised their ancestors, I replied, "Over my dead body." I stand by my words.

There is a scene in Monty Python and the Holy Grail where King Arthur encounters a knight dressed in black. The knight refuses to let Arthur pass, even after he explains that he is King of all the Britons. The ensuing duel is fairly evenly matched at first until Arthur strikes a blow which removes the black knight's left arm.

Undaunted the black night says, "Tis but a scratch. I've had worse," and continues to fight. Moments later his right arm is lopped off to which he responds, "It's just a flesh wound."

Arthur is prepared to end the battle there and go on his way, but the persistent knight begins kicking at the king, still refusing to let him pass by. Arthur reluctantly swings his sword again, chopping off one of armless man's legs.

"I'm invincible! The black knight always triumphs," the man declares, hopping on one foot and clumsily bumping into the king. Needing to continue on his journey, Arthur finally concedes and slices off the knight's other leg. As he sits on the ground, armless and legless, watching the king and coconut clapping squire walk by, the determined knight calls out, "Oh, I see. Running away, eh? Come back here and take what's coming to you! I'll bite your legs off!"

The scene above reminds me a lot of the story of Pharaoh. When Moses first enters his court, we could certainly excuse the king for presuming an advantage. After all, he was the king of the most powerful empire in the world at that time. Moses was a Midianite shepherd speaking on behalf of Hebrew slaves. From Pharaoh's perspective, there is no reason for him to question his assumption that he decidedly held the upper hand.

When Aaron's staff becomes a snake, Pharaoh's magicians counter which gives him no reason to re-evaluate his point of view. As the first couple of plagues hit, the king's magicians do their best to keep up, but each time, the best they can come up with is an inferior facsimile. This should have been enough to cause the king to think twice, but it didn't. By the time plague number four arrives, the magicians themselves are telling Pharaoh that they're up against a God more powerful than they. But their counsel falls on deaf ears.

By plague number seven, many of the Egyptians are hedging their bets on the side of the Hebrew's God, but not Pharaoh. He not only refuses to believe he is holding an incredibly weak hand but seems to be doubling down at every opportunity. There are occasional moments where the king seems to grasp who he's up against, but as soon as things return to normal he reverts to egotistical defiance.

Even after the tenth and most horrific plague, Pharaoh still finds the nerve to chase after the Hebrews. Even when he sees the waters parted and the people walking across on dry ground he refuses to acknowledge that maybe, just maybe, he's a little out of his league.

Most of us look at Pharaoh's stubbornness and view it as foolishness. At some point, you would think he'd realize he was horribly outgunned and cut his losses while he could. But he refuses to relent. The waters are made murkier by the repeated statements claiming, “The Lord hardened Pharaoh’s heart.”

This seems wrong at best and cruel at worst. How is it possible that God would harden Pharaoh’s heart to prevent the release of the Hebrews and heap further suffering upon the Egyptians? That doesn’t seem right. That seems to violate the concept of free will. That doesn’t seem like something God should do.

God tells Moses, prior to his first encounter with the Egyptian king, that He will harden Pharaoh’s heart (Exodus 7:3). The text itself claims several times throughout the story that the Lord did exactly that, (Exodus 9:12; 10:1,20,27; 11:10; 14:4,8). However, it should be noted that the text also states repeatedly that Pharaoh hardened his own heart, (Exodus 8:15,32; 9:34). On other occasions, the text uses the passive voice to state that Pharaoh’s heart was hardened, without identifying who or what caused this hardening to happen, (Exodus 7:13,14,22; 8:19; 9:7,35).

As such, it would seem that Pharaoh’s hard-heartedness was the result of several factors.

- The actions of God

- The allowance of God
- The king's self-serving choices
- The king's stubborn and egotistical personality

Which, when you think about it, makes perfect sense. If I'm being honest, those are the same factors that cause spiritual hardness in my own heart too.

God doesn't do what I want, doesn't do things the way I think they should be done, doesn't prevent what I think should be prevented, or doesn't bring about what I think should happen, and my heart hardens. I get mad at God. I shake my fist at the sky. I grumble under my breath.

And God, holding true to His promise to let me make my own decisions, choices, and mistakes, allows me to go down that path. He might put up huge caution signs or send numerous friendly reminders, but if I really want to go there, He'll let me go.

Having rejected God's wisdom and direction I am left at the mercy of my own intelligence and intuition. As a general rule, without divine guidance, both of these tend to skew to the selfish side of things. I like the things that benefit me. I prefer things that work to, what I perceive to be, my advantage. I pursue whatever I think will get me what I want.

You see, I, much like Pharaoh, usually think I know what is right. I'm generally convinced I know what is best, especially when it comes to my own welfare. Even when my decisions don't pan out and my choices backfire, I am highly prone to grit my teeth, dig in my heels and stubbornly forge ahead rather than admit that I might possibly have been, ~~wrong~~ not entirely correct.

The ten plagues make God seem to be rather harsh, particularly the last one. However, in many ways, they actually show God's great patience and determination to win over someone who had set their heart against Him. When you consider that God could have, with a single word, wiped Pharaoh and every trace of the Egyptian empire off the face of the map, gnats, flies and frogs seems like a pretty tolerant approach.

The story of Pharaoh is not about a God who is impulsive and will obliterate anyone who challenges Him on a whim. It is the story of a God who is radically committed to keeping His promise to those who are faithfully following Him and, at the same time, do everything within His power to persuade those who have set themselves against Him that they are on a collision course with their own destruction in a desperate hope they will reconsider before it's too late.

> *The Lord is not slow in keeping his promise, as some understand slowness. Instead, he is patient with you, not wanting anyone to perish, but everyone to come to repentance. (2 Peter 3:9 NIV)*

HELLO
MY NAME IS
Joshua

Going in Circles

Hello, my name is Joshua. My story begins a long time ago in a country far, far away. I was born in Egypt, you see, but I'm not an Egyptian. I was a Hebrew, as they called us. The word itself means to cross over, or pass through, but to the Egyptians it meant one thing only: slave labor.

When I was in my late teens, God raised up a great leader who went head to head with Pharaoh again and again. Eventually, God persuaded the king of Egypt, not only to give us our freedom but clothes, livestock, gold, and silver too! All the descendants of Israel, as we called ourselves, marched out of Egypt and through the Red Sea. Yes, I said *through* the Red Sea.

God fed us on our journey, by causing magic bread to appear on the ground every morning, quail to land in the camp at night and water to spring right out of the rocks when no other source could be found. He gave us His instructions for living and led us right to the doorstep of Canaan. For centuries, our people had referred to Canaan as "The

Promised Land" because God had told our ancestor Abraham long ago that it would all belong to him and his descendants.

Of course, there is much more to the story, but it's not really my story to tell. That honor belongs to Moses, or Old Mo, as I liked to call him. Mo was the one who led us out of Egypt, across the wilderness to the very borders of Canaan. He was a tremendous leader and I was blessed to eventually become his right-hand man. However, Old Mo would be the first to tell you he wasn't anyone special. He often reminded me, "None of this could have happened, none of it, if the LORD had not done it."

We camped out in the wilderness about a hundred miles south of Canaan, and Mo told each of our twelve tribes or clans, to pick one representative each to be part of a covert survey team that would go inspect the land to see what we were up against. My clan selected me. The twelve of us snuck into Canaan and checked out as much of the land as we could. After forty days, we returned to camp and reported what we had seen.

"It was like nothing we have ever seen!" Palti exclaimed.

"It's a land flowing with milk and honey," Ammiel added. "Everything God promised it would be, and more!"

"Check out these grapes," Igal beamed, holding up a branch we had cut off and brought back with us. "They're HUGE!"

"Wonderful," Old Mo cheered. "We will make our plans to advance immediately."

"NO!" several of the men shouted in unison.

"Don't get me wrong," Geuel explained. "It is everything these guys have described, but we can't go."

"Well, why not?"

"The people are big and strong. They make us look like kids. They have armor and weapons. Their cities are fortified with huge walls and sturdy gates. We won't last five seconds against these guys. They'll squash us like ants. We'll all be wiped out."

That's when my buddy Caleb spoke up. "Simmer down boys. There's no need to overreact here. God has brought us this far, He's not going to let us down now. We should attack immediately and the LORD will be victorious!"

Old Mo and his brother Aaron decided to sleep on it before making a decision. However, that night, as you might imagine, the stories of the land of Canaan were shared all over camp and the people came to their own conclusion about what should be done. By the time morning came, much to Mo's dismay, the people's mind was made up and nothing he said could convince them to follow God into Canaan.

The LORD spoke to Mo and said, "If these people do not want to enter the land I have promised them, then I will grant them their wish. Not one person over the age of twenty, except Caleb and Joshua, will enter Canaan. The people will wander aimlessly in the wilderness for forty years. But I will keep my covenant with Abraham, and their children will receive the land I have promised.

And that's what happened. For four decades, the people wandered in the desert. But even in those years, God kept us safe and well fed. Our clothes never wore out and our feet never blistered. Forty years later we arrived on the shores of the Jordan river, just across from the city of Jericho. Old Mo, now one hundred and twenty years old, appointed me his successor and then passed away.

So, there we stood, poised to enter God's promised land…again. Of course, it was only Caleb and myself who had actually been there before. Everyone else in the camp was too young to remember or wasn't even born the last time we were in this position. Once again, we were faced with a choice.

I sent two men into the city to investigate their defenses and search for possible weaknesses. The Jerichoans were on high alert. They had seen our tents across the river and they weren't taking any chances. Bear in mind, we had 600,000 able-bodied men to fight and at least as many women and children as well. Tough to miss a group like that camped on your doorstep. Word got out that our spies had infiltrated the city and the men of Jericho turned into Tommy Lee Jones and conducted a hard target search of every shop, residence, warehouse, farmhouse, henhouse, outhouse and doghouse. Our boys would have been caught too, had it not been for the kindness of a lady who hid them in the red light district and then snuck them out of town.

When the men return they reported that the land was very much as I had remembered it: rich and luscious. Unfortunately, the people were still big, strong and well armed. After the incident with our spies, the city of Jericho closed its doors and barred its gates making it impossible to enter. But the men told me something else, something that kind of surprised me, although it really shouldn't have.

"The LORD has surely given the whole land into our hands," they said. "All the people are melting in fear because of us!"

We all swelled with confidence at the spies' report, but then, God delivered his battle plan. "Tomorrow, I want you to take the Ark of the Covenant and have the people march around the walls of Jericho."

"Won't their archers pick us off like sitting ducks?" I asked.

"No," the LORD answered. "You won't be sitting, you will be marching. And I will keep you safe."

"Okay Lord, then what?"

"Return to camp and rest up for the next day."

"Why, what happens the next day?"

"You march around the city again."

"You want us to march around the city two days in a row?"

"No. I want you to march around the city seven days in a row."

"Really? There must be something more to this plan."

"Right you are Josh," God answered. "On the seventh day, I want you to march around the city ... wait for it ... seven times."

"And then what, the walls will just fall down?" I asked incredulously.

"No, don't be silly. After the seventh lap on the seventh day, I want the priests to blow their horns and the people to shout as loud as they can, and *then* the walls will fall down."

It was, without a doubt, a crazy plan, but Old Mo had taught me long ago there was no point in arguing with God. So, I told the plan to the rest of the people and assured them the LORD would give us the victory. Of course, it wasn't lost on anyone that the people who had just spent forty years hiking around in the desert were about to conquer a fortified city by walking around it.

We woke up the next morning and we all marched around the city of Jericho, just like God had instructed us to do. True to His word, God kept us safe. Not a single spear, arrow or stone came down from upon the city wall. All week long we made our daily trek around Jericho without incident.

On the seventh day, we walked around the city seven times. We all shouted and blew our trumpets and the mighty walls of the city collapsed upon themselves. The city was exposed and vulnerable. If the people had been scared of us before, they were absolutely terrified now. Out fighting men went in and conquered the city easily.

Not only had God kept His covenant to deliver the promised land into our hands, but He did it in jaw (and wall) dropping style.

I was recently told that peppermint oil is an effective treatment for a sinus infection. I had never heard of this remedy before, but I thought, “I suppose putting some peppermint oil in a nice cup of tea might help” – although to be honest, I’d give most of the credit to the tea. However, when I was told the treatment involved not drinking the oil but rather, slathering it on the soles of your feet, I was more than a little skeptical. The idea that oil on my feet can somehow remove mucus from my head seemed unlikely, to say the least. I see no obvious connection between cause and effect. Which I think is what Joshua must have felt when God explained His plan for conquering Jericho.

When God tells the Israelites they will conquer the city by walking around it 13 times, I'm sure it was tough to believe. It would be like if I shared my breakthrough weight loss strategy: wearing colored socks, or told you about my plan to get rich quick by eating tacos. Most of you would say, "What does one thing have to do with another?" Some of you even had to go back to read that sentence again, because it made so little sense to you the first time. I'm certain when Joshua revealed God's plan to the people there were plenty of people saying, "Umm, excuse me. Could you please repeat that? I must not have heard you correctly."

As far-fetched as this battle plan seems, it is far more preposterous than you realize. Archaeologists tell us that Jericho is one of the oldest cities in all of history. It had been there a long time before Joshua & Co. showed up. It was built in a coveted location and the land produced rich crops, and thus lots of people wanted to stake claim to it. This meant the people who lived there had to be ready to defend it, so they built a wall.

Perhaps I should clarify a bit. They didn't build *a wall* – they built *walls*. Three of them to be exact. The first was a 12-15 foot stone retaining wall around the base of the city. On top of that was a second wall made of mud bricks. It was six feet thick and as much as 26 feet tall. Behind these walls was a steep embankment leading up to the city itself. At the top of the slope was a second mudbrick wall similar in dimension to the lower wall. Not only was the top of the inner wall an estimated 60 feet above ground level, but even if an invader somehow managed to scale the outer walls, they would be easy targets for the archers above as they tried to make their way up the embankment and scale or break through the upper wall.

To make matters worse, the Israelites had lost the element of surprise. The people of Jericho had seen them coming a long way off. They could see the camp from atop their city walls. The spies Joshua had sent into the city had been spotted and almost captured. The people of Jericho knew the Israelites were coming, so the city was shut up tight and no one was allowed in or out. And let's not forget the Israelites had just spent the last forty years wandering in the wilderness which meant they had no siege towers, catapults or battering rams – just some bows, spears and swords. That's it.

What chance did they have against such a highly fortified city like Jericho? None and that was kind of the point. God wanted it to be clear, to the Israelites and to everyone else, that this victory belonged to Him. This was all His doing. His promise was being fulfilled by His power.

I used to think walking around the city day after day was meant to be some kind of endurance test for the Israelites. As if God was trying to make sure they really wanted it. But that's the way I think. God's not like that. As it turns out, the circumference of the city, the distance the Israelites had to walk each day, was less than half a mile (2/3 km). That's roughly the size of an average city block. Even on day seven when the Israelites made seven full laps, it was only a total of 2.8 miles (4.7 km). Most of us could casually knock that off in less than an hour.

So, what was the point? It obviously wasn't a test of Israel's physical strength. It certainly wasn't meant to be intimidating to the people of Jericho. Confusing, yes. Scary, no. I think the point was twofold.

First, as mentioned earlier, this story is about displaying the greatness of God. No one is ever going to be conned into thinking that somehow the Israelites walking a combined total of a whopping 5.4 miles (8.7 km) made one lick of difference to how this battle turned out. God chose one of the most heavily fortified and well-armed cities as the place where the people of Israel would make their entrance into the land of Canaan and then He handed it over to them.

And yet, God didn't want His people to sit on the sidelines and watch. He wanted them to participate, even if their contribution was relatively minute in the grand scheme of things. God wanted them to be a part of what He was doing.

Moreover, actually going out and walking around the city, day after day, following God's instructions even when they didn't seem logical or practical; even when the plan didn't particularly make sense to them; even when they couldn't see how what they were doing mattered; even when for 12.9 laps it looked like absolutely nothing at all was happening was an unmistakable display of their trust – not in what they were doing, but in the One who told them to do it.

Which is where I think this story really hits home for us: Are we willing to do what they did? Are we willing to walk the way God has called us to walk? Step after step, day after day, year in and year out? Even when we don't totally understand the reasoning? Even when those around us tell us it's foolish? Even when we don't see the pay off right away?

My favorite verse in this story says: *Then the LORD said to Joshua, "See, I have delivered Jericho into your hands, along with its kings and its fighting men."* Can't you just see Joshua standing on top of a pile of rubble as the people are flooding into the city in victory? What a triumphant moment!

The only catch is, this verse comes *before* the battle. In fact, it comes before God even tells Joshua the plan. This statement comes when all Joshua knows is that there is a heavily armed and impenetrable city on high alert, just waiting for the Israelites to dare to make a move.

If I was Joshua I think I might have replied, "No, God, I don't actually see that. I see huge walls. I see barred gates. I see armed soldiers." But that's not what God saw. God saw victory. God saw deliverance. God saw fulfilled promise. And He told Joshua, "I know things don't always look the same to you, but I need you to trust me on this one."

I don't think that was easy for Joshua. I don't think it was easy for the rest of Israel either. I know it's not always easy for us. But that's what God calls us to, not for His sake, but for ours. As the writer of Psalm 37 reminds us so well:

> *Trust in the LORD and do good. In whatever situation, you find yourself in. When things are going well and when they're not. When you can see know how it will all work out and when you don't. When you can see clearly what God is about to do and when all you can see is the wall. Just keep walking. Step by step. Day by day. Moment by moment. Trust in the LORD and do good, and leave the rest up to Him.*

HELLO
MY NAME IS
Balaam

Way, Hey, and Away We Go

Hello, my name is Balaam. I have to confess, I'm likely not the kind of guy you think I am. If I told you I lived during the time of Moses and delivered messages from God to people you'd probably say, "Oh, he must be a prophet. He must be one of the good guys." In truth, I'm probably neither one. In fact, and this might surprise you, I wasn't even an Israelite. Nope, I was an Assyrian. I lived on the shores of the Euphrates River in a city called Pethor. I had never even met an Israelite before.

In my hometown of Pethor, I was what you'd call a fortune teller. I got to be quite good at it too. People would pay me to predict their future. I did blessings and curses too, for a modest fee of course. Fortunately for me, most of my predictions came true. Most of the people I cursed had bad luck and most of the people I blessed had good luck. I became a bit of celebrity, not just in my hometown, but across the entire region.

So, there I was, just chillaxing on the shores of the Euphrates when this group of guys walked up to me. I could tell two things just by looking at them. First of all, they clearly weren't locals. No self-respecting Assyrian would be caught dead wearing a tunic like that. Only a Canaanite would dare to wear something so garish. And second, they appeared to people of some importance. Not kings, but something close to it.

"We are representatives of the elders of Midian and King Balak of Moab," they introduced themselves. "We have been sent to employ your *special talents* to deal with a certain *situation* we have going on at home."

They proceeded to open up a chest full of gold, silver, and gems to be offered as payment. The price certainly looked right, so I asked, "What exactly is it you need me to do for you?"

"There is a tribe of people coming out of Egypt, headed toward our territory. They call themselves Israelites. It is a large group and they will consume all the resources of our land like locusts if something is not done to stop them. King Balak wants you to put a curse on them."

"Well, I don't know. Give me the night to sleep on in it." This is always my go-to response because nine times out of ten people will increase their offer the next morning if they think I might say no. That night I went through my usual divination routine, but this time was different. This time God spoke to me. I mean *the* God.

He said, "Don't do it. The people they want you to curse are MY people. My blessing is upon them."

The next morning, I told the men that I could not curse the Israelites. As much as I could use the cash, there was no way I was going against *the* God. On cue, they offered me more money, but I told them I wouldn't do it even for all the cats in Egypt. So, they left and returned to Moab.

About two months later another group of men approached me. It only took a glance to know that these guys were VIPs – very impressive princes. King Balak had sent out the big guns this time. And twice as many of them offering twice as much money for the same simple job – curse the Israelites. I told them straight up that I wouldn't dare go against the instructions I had received from *the* God.

Then they said, "Name your price!"

"Well ... I guess it couldn't hurt to ask again." I replied. "Come back in the morning and I'll let you know." I once again went through my ritual and waited for an answer. I'll be honest, I was really hoping the answer would be "yes" because they were offering me a boatload of money.

Finally, *the* God spoke, "Alright. If you really want to you can go, but just bear in mind, you can only say what I want you to say." I eagerly agreed, not fully realizing exactly what that meant.

I rose early the next morning, saddled my donkey and headed off with the princes of Moab. Right off the bat, we ran into trouble. Suddenly, out of nowhere, my donkey veered off to the left and wandered off the path out into the middle of the field. Strange behavior from what had always been a reliable animal.

I beat the donkey until it returned to the path and continued on my way. It wasn't long before she veered off again, this time to the right, crushing my foot against the stone wall of a vineyard. I beat the donkey again, to get it back into the middle of the path.

A while later we came to a narrow spot in the road where there was just enough room for us to squeeze through single file. After everyone else had gone through the bottleneck, I followed at the rear of the group. Or at least I tried to. My donkey stopped right at the narrow area and would not move an inch. I kicked and prodded and beat her like, well, like a rented mule, and still, she wouldn't budge.

"Hey! What's the big idea?" a voice shouted. It caught me by surprise because everyone else had gone through the narrow pass ahead of me. "What have I ever done to you to deserve getting beaten half to death"

"You're making me look stupid in front of the paying customers," I sneered. And then it hit me: I'm having a conversation with my donkey.

"Well, did you ever think there might be a reason?" the donkey asked

It was right about then that my eyes were opened and I could see what the donkey had been looking at all day long: an angel standing directly in front of us with his sword drawn. It was a terrifying sight.

"I'm am here to warn you," the angel said. "The path you're on is a reckless one. I'd turn back now if I were you."

Then the angel disappeared. "Boy, I'm sure glad *he's* gone," I said to the donkey. "Can we please go *now*?" We continued on our way to Moab without further incident, but I think I must have hurt the donkey's feelings because she has been giving me the silent treatment ever since.

About twenty days later I arrived in Moab. "King Balak," I said. "I want you to know how much I appreciate your very generous offer, but I think it's only fair to warn you that god, *the* God, has told me I can only say the words He puts in my mouth." It always helps to start off with a disclaimer, just in case something goes wrong. I instructed the king to build seven altars and sacrifice seven bulls and seven rams upon them. Then I stood in front of the altars to curse the Israelites, but much to my shock and the king's dismay, the words that came out of my mouth were ones of blessing.

"What's the big idea?" the king protested. "I'm paying you to curse them, not bless them!"

"Umm, I think it's this location," I said, scrambling for a plausible excuse. "There must be some bad mojo here or something. Maybe we should try again someplace else."

Well, to make a long story short, an additional three locations, twenty-one altars with twenty-one rams and twenty-one bulls, three blessings and exactly zero curses later, King Balak had heard enough. "You're fired," he declared. "Go home, you fraud. You're not getting a cent from me."

"In my defense, I did tell you I could only say what *the* God told me to," I offered weakly. "But, maybe this thing doesn't have to be a total bust. I have an idea." I suggested that the king gather up the most beautiful women in his kingdom and send them down to near where the Israelites would be passing by. Your women can seduce the Israelite men and once they've got them hooked, they can persuade the Israelites to worship your gods. Then *the* God will surely reject them and they will be vulnerable to your attacks or my curses.

And that is exactly what King Balak did. In the end, it worked like a charm: twenty-four thousand of the Israelites turned away from *the* God and I laughed all the way to the bank.

Last summer I took my boys to camp for the first time. On the way, we were discussing all the rules that they needed to remember:

- Stay away from the girl's cabins
- Don't go in the water without an adult supervisor
- Always wear a life jacket in a boat
- Don't go in the woods

When we got to that last one, my ever-so-helpful eldest son added, "Because there are bears that will eat you."

I said, "Yes, there are bears."

Later that night, as we settled into our sleeping bags in the tent, my youngest son said, very matter-of-factly, "Dad, you should have told me there were bears before I said, 'Yes', to coming here."

I suppose I probably should have. And if he had really wanted to bail at that point, I guess it would have been my fault for not making him fully informed of what he was getting himself into.

Balaam had no such excuse. God told him right up front and in no uncertain terms, "These are *my* people. They have *my* blessing. Under no circumstances may you curse them." However, when Balak's men return a second time offering more money, Balaam asks God again. God replies, "Was I not clear the first time? Fine, you can go with them if you really want to, but remember you can only say what I tell you to say, (and if you were paying attention you would know that I will bless them, not curse them). I guess, as long as you are going in with your eyes wide open: Knowing what is going to happen; Knowing how your employer is going to feel about it – Knock yourself out, but don't say I didn't warn you."

Balaam went anyway, which is why God was angry with him. In truth, I think God was as much disappointed as He was angry. I can only presume that Balaam thought there was some way to get around God's directions. Maybe he hoped God would change His mind, or at least not be watching when he went to pronounce the curse.

It's worth noting that God doesn't send a lightning bolt to zap Balaam and the princes of Moab. Instead, He tries the subtle approach first. God sends an angel to block Balaam's path three times. The donkey sees the angel and tries to veer away. But Balaam is so determined to do what he has planned he beats the poor mule within an inch of its life, trying to force it to get back on the road to Moab. Let's just pause here and state the obvious: if your donkey sees what God is doing before you do – you have a problem. God even goes so far as having the donkey speak and having the angel appear to Balaam and essentially say, "You're making a huge mistake. Turn back now while you still can." Friends, if an angel (or donkey) tells you your making a huge mistake and you should turn back, please turn back!

Let's try to put this in context. Our family travels to the States every year to visit my wife's family. Just imagine if God spoke to me before our last trip and said, "Don't go." I'm pretty sure that would cause me to think twice about making the trek. Nonetheless, my wife would tell me again how much she really wanted to go see her family. So, I would pray about it again. However, in response, God clearly replied, "You can go if you want to, but I'm telling you now: it's not going to end well."

Let's say, for argument sake, we decided to go anyway. However, as soon as we got on the highway our car started spontaneously veering off the road. Undeterred, I would drive back out of the ditch and keep going. Finally, after several more ditch dives, the car broke down and stopped altogether. No matter what I tried I couldn't get it going again. As I was pounding on the steering wheel and the dash in frustration, the radio turned itself on and a voice rang out of the speakers saying, "Leave me alone! I've been a reliable car for ten years!"

Just then, an angel appeared near the front bumper and said, "Don't go. You're only asking for trouble."

When the angel disappeared, I called you up, told you everything that had happened and asked what you thought I should do. What would your advice be? Unless you really don't like me, your advice would likely be: turn around immediately and go home!

God warns Balaam repeatedly. He gives Balaam every opportunity to turn around and go back. But Balaam goes to Moab anyway. Bear in mind it was a twenty-day trip. There was plenty of time to reconsider. Plenty of time to ponder his decision. Plenty of time to think better, wise up and turn back...but he didn't.

I think the big take away from Balaam's story is the startling and sobering truth that, if you are determined to do so, God will let you go to Moab. Yes, He'll warn you of the dangers and urge you not to go. He'll put obstacles in your way to prompt you to alter your course and turn back, but in the end, if you really want to go to Moab, God will let you go. In other words, God will caution you against poor choices, but He won't fully prevent you from making them. God will try to talk you out of bad decisions, but He won't force you to do things His way.

Balaam's story reminds me a lot of a story Jesus told in Luke 15. It is most commonly known as the Prodigal Son or the

Lost Son, but it could just as easily be called the Forgiving Father or the Bitter Brother. The story goes like this: A man has two sons and the youngest asks for his inheritance. I'm sure the father would have tried to reason with his son; tried to warn him; tried to alter his course, but in the end, the father gives his son what he asked for. The son goes off to a far away country and blows it all on big parties and doing all the stuff his dad has always told him he should never do.

Eventually, the money runs out, as it always does. His friends disappear and the good times stop rolling. Now he's left to deal with the harsh reality and consequences of the choices he's made. The exact same consequences, no doubt, his father had tried to warn him about before he left home. The father knew what would happen. He tried to warn his son, but in the end, he let him go to Moab.

I think God still does the same thing with us today. He gives us His instructions. He warns us when we're headed into dangerous territory. He puts obstacles in our path to try and alter our course. He pleads with us to reconsider, but in the end, if we're determined to do so, He will let us go to Moab.

If we choose to

- Lie, cheat or steal – He'll let us
- Abuse substances or relationships – He'll let us

- Be bitter, angry, mean or spiteful – He'll let us
- Be greedy, covetous or selfish – He'll let us
- Hate instead of love – He'll let us

Even though it will break His heart, He'll let us do it. And in the end, just like Balaam and the Prodigal Son, we'll be faced with the consequences of disregarding His advice.

Of course, those of you who are familiar with the story of the Prodigal Son know that the son ends up in a farmyard eating pig slop, but the story doesn't end there. In what might be one of the most fitting phrases in the Bible, Jesus explains, *"When he came to his senses," (Luke 15:17a NIV).* Isn't that the perfect term? When he came to his senses... When he realized what he had done... When it finally clicked that he had gone down the wrong path... When he grasped what a mistake he had made... When he saw what a mess he had made of things... When it dawned on him that his dad was right...he decided, *"I will set out and go back to my father." (Luke 15:18a NIV)*

When the son returned home the father was waiting. Not just waiting, he was watching – scanning the horizon for the son's return. And when he saw the son, finally headed in the right direction, the father ran to him, hugged and kissed him, and welcomed him back home. Just like God has always done for me. Just like God will always do for you.

You know, when you think about it, it's rather fitting that Balaam's story features a donkey. Donkeys are notorious for their stubbornness; their independence; their determination to go where they want, when they want, at whatever speed they want. And that pretty much sums up the attitude of Balaam too, doesn't it? At times, it has summed up my attitude and I suspect there have been moments when it could be a fairly apt description of your attitude as well.

Balaam's story teaches us that if you want to be as stubborn as a mule and go your own way despite God's warnings and obstacles – God will let you go. And when you finally come to your senses, God will be standing there with arms wide open, waiting for you to come back home!

HELLO
MY NAME IS
Gideon

I Just got Fleeced

Hello, my name is Gideon. You may not know who I am because I'm not a super-famous guy like David or Daniel. In fact, I'm kind of a nobody really. Actually, that's exactly what I told God the first time we talked too. But He wasn't listening. He had other plans of His own.

I guess to really explain things, I need to back up a bit. You see, my people, the Israelites, had been getting bullied by the neighboring nation of Midian for seven long years. The Midianites were just plain mean. They would invade our country at will, taking all our crops and livestock. What they didn't take they would burn or kill which left us with pretty much nothing.

We didn't have an army of our own so we had no means of fighting them off or defending ourselves. I suspect God would have come and rescued us from the Midianites if we had just asked, but we didn't. We were too busy worshipping the Canaanite gods, particularly the sun god Baal and his consort the moon goddess Asherah. Ironically Baal was a god of agricultural prosperity and Asherah was a goddess of success in battle. You would think that after seven years of invasions and stolen crops we would have taken the hint, but somehow, we didn't.

Anyway, there I was one day, threshing wheat in our family wine press. I know what you're thinking: Isn't a wine press for crushing grapes, not threshing wheat? Well, yes, yes it is. And I can confirm that threshing wheat in a wine press is an utterly miserable endeavor. It is small and cramped. There's no room to properly beat the sheaves and you can't throw the stalks up in the air like you normally would. It was only a matter of minutes before I was swelteringly hot and the air was thick with dust and tiny bits of chaff.

However, if I had threshed my wheat out in the open I ran the risk of the Midianites seeing me. If that happened they would know that our crop was ready to harvest and a whole swarm of them would have been on our doorstep before you could say "Bar mitzvah." They'd take what they wanted and torch the rest.

So, there I was, sweaty, tired and dirty, threshing wheat in a winepress when BAM! an angel appeared and said, "The LORD is with you mighty warrior!"

I said, "Dude, I think you've got the wrong winepress."

Speaking through the angel, God said, "I am calling you, Gideon, to help me free my people from the oppression of the Midianites."

"That sounds great, but I'm pretty sure I'm not your guy. I'm pretty much a nobody. My tribe is one of the least in all of Israel. In fact, we're not even a full-fledged tribe, we're a half tribe. Not only that, but my clan is the smallest in our entire tribe and in my family, I'm pretty much the runt of the litter if you know what I mean."

God said, "I know, but I'll be with you."

To be honest, I wasn't sure what to say next, so I asked the angel to just wait right there for a moment. I ran to the kitchen and grabbed some bread, meat and heated up some broth. I took the food out to the angel and he said, "Put the bread and meat on that stone over there. Now pour the broth on top."

I assumed this meant he wasn't pleased with my meager offering, but then, he reached out with the tip of his staff, tapped the rock and BOOM, the stone burst into flame, incinerating the bread and meat completely! I turned around and the angel had disappeared

I said, “Okay God, you got me. What do we do now?”

God said, “First things, first. We need to get rid of all the altars of Baal and statues of Asherah.”

That very night I gathered together a group of guys and we destroyed my family’s altar and Asherah pole – under the safety of the cover of darkness of course. Then I built a new altar to the LORD in their place. As you might expect, it didn’t take long for our neighbors to figure out what had happened and who had done it.

The next morning an angry mob of people knocked on our front door. They were upset by what I had done and were worried my actions would offend the gods and bring misfortune and bad luck upon our city – not like they had been giving us good luck thus far anyway. Thankfully it was my dad who answered the door, not me.

“If Baal is so upset about it,” my father told the men, “Let him do something about it himself.” After the crowd had dispersed my dad gave me the nickname Jerub-Baal (which means “Let Baal deal with him”). He’s called me that, every day since.

Now, building altars was one thing, but taking on the Midianites was another thing altogether, so I asked God for a little confirmation. I told God that I would leave a piece of fleece out on the ground overnight. If He really wants *me* to lead His people against Midian, in the morning there should be dew on the fleece, but not the rest of the ground

God said, “Okay.”

Sure enough, the next morning the ground was bone dry, but the fleece was drenched. Not just covered with dew, but soaking wet. When I wrung it out the water filled up an entire bowl. Then it occurred to me, maybe the ground was covered with dew earlier, but it dried up faster than the dew on the fleece.

Yeah, I know it was a long shot, but truth be told, I was kind of looking for a way out of this whole thing. So, I told God, “Let’s try that one more time. I’m going to put the exact same fleece in the exact same place, but, this time make the ground wet and the fleece dry.”

God said, “Done.”

The next morning, as I walked across the lawn, the water squished under my sandals, soaking my feet with each step. I picked the fleece up out of the puddle it was sitting in and, you guessed it, not a drop.

That very day I put out the call for men to come fight against Midian and 32,000 showed up, which frankly was far more than I expected. Then God spoke to me and said, "You have too many men."

I replied, "You do know it is still about 100,000 less than the Midianites have, don't you?"

"103,000," God said. "But who's counting? You have too many men. Tell anyone who is scared they can go home."

I did, and 22,000 men left. I took the remaining 10,000 men down by the river to get organized and train for battle. God said, "You've still got too many men." Then he had us do this test based on how the men drank water from the river, which I still don't totally understand, but the bottom line was 9700 were sent home and only 300 of us remained.

That's when God shared His battle plan with us. We each took a torch, a trumpet and a clay pot – not your typical weapons to say the least. We lit the torches and put them inside the pots to hide their light. Then, in the middle of the night, we went out and surrounded the Midianite camp. All at once, everyone broke their pots, blew their trumpets and shouted at the top of their lungs.

I have to admit; it was kind of a rush! I totally felt like Joshua at the battle of Jericho! The Midianites woke up in alarm and thought they were being invaded by a massive army. They all scrambled out of bed and in the darkness and confusion started attacking each other. The majority of their troops were taken out by their own men. A small group escaped and we quickly chased them down.

The Midianites were routed. Israel was free. I don't mean to toot my own horn, but it was an incredible victory.

Much like an epic Hollywood movie, the climax of Gideon's story seems to be the great battle scene. And much like a Hollywood movie, that is where we often focus the majority of our attention and understandably so. After all, it is a rather compelling scene. It's the three hundred versus the one hundred and thirty-five thousand! Farmers versus warriors. Clay pots and torches versus swords and armor. The oppressed good guys versus the evil tyrants. But it seems to me that, in this case, the battle is just the icing on the cake. The really interesting part of this story happens long before the battle begins.

When we first meet Gideon, he is secretly threshing wheat in a wine press. He is just a shy farm boy, from a small family in a minor tribe. He is far more Clarke Kent than he is Superman. Even by his own assessment, Gideon isn't much and probably isn't capable of much. However, God shows up and calls Gideon which changes the plot. The interesting thing is that God calls Gideon not based on who he is, but rather based on who he can be with God. Gideon's resume alone would certainly not have gotten him an interview, let alone land the job. Despite his lack of qualifications, this story starts with God calling Gideon a mighty warrior and it ends with Gideon actually being a mighty warrior. Generally speaking, we usually expect things to be the other way around.

The most fascinating part of this story is not that God answered His people's cry for help and delivered them from the oppression of the Midianites. We saw that coming a mile away, right? That's what God does. The intriguing part of this story is that if you had traveled Israel looking for a leader to raise up an army to take on the Midianites, I'm almost certain you would not have picked Gideon. He probably wouldn't have made your short list. He may not even have made your long list.

But perhaps that shouldn't surprise us. After all, look at some of the other people God called. When God called Moses, in Exodus 3, to lead His people out of Egypt, what was Moses' response? He said, "Who am I that I should lead them? Why should they listen to me? I'm not an eloquent speaker. Can't you send someone else?"

When Samuel went to the house of Jesse to call a new king to rule over God's people Jesse paraded out all his sons one by one. Samuel passed on all of them and finally asked Jesse if he had any more children. Jesse replied, "Well, you know, there is one more – David. He's just a kid though. He's out playing his harp and watching the sheep. You don't want him. Why don't you take another look at Eliab? He's big and strong and tough. Or how about Abinadab? He's smart as a tack that one."

Or how about the prophets? Isaiah said, *"Woe to me! I am ruined! For I am a man of unclean lips, and I live among a people of unclean lips," (Isaiah 6:5a NIV)*. Jeremiah told God, *"O Sovereign LORD, I can't speak for you! I'm too young!" (Jeremiah 1:6 NLT)*. And let's not forget about Jonah! He felt so underqualified he attempted to sail so far away that God wouldn't be able to find him.

And when God is ready to send His Son to earth, who would you chose to be the guardians of the infant Messiah? Perhaps someone wealthy who can adequately provide for him. Maybe a priest and his wife who can train Him in the scriptures. It would make sense for it to be someone of power who can provide Him with opportunities and advantages. We might pick someone of influence in Jerusalem who can get Him the exposure He deserves. But that's not who God selects. He chooses a teenage girl and her carpenter fiancée living in a backwoods little town in the middle of nowhere.

Even the people Jesus, Himself, called to be His closest followers weren't from among the rich and famous. They did not belong to high society or come from the upper levels of academia. They were fisherman and tax collectors. They were zealots and rabble rousers. They were unknown and, in the case of Nathaniel, guys who apparently had nothing better to do than sit around under a fig tree all day.

You cannot read through very many pages of the Bible without realizing God will call pretty much anyone to join Him in His mission. He will invite anyone to have a relationship with Him. Which means, whatever it is you think disqualifies you from being called by God; whatever you think makes you inadequate to be used by Him to accomplish His purposes; in whatever way you think you don't measure up enough to catch God's attention, I've got news for you: you've already caught God's attention. He is eager to work through you. In fact, He's been calling you to join Him for a while now.

Of course, we could look at the story of Gideon and say, "This doesn't make sense. It doesn't add up. How can you give an underqualified person an overwhelming job and expect things to turn out as anything but a disaster?" And perhaps you feel that way about getting involved in God's work yourself. Perhaps you think there are more qualified people than you. Maybe you feel like he's more capable or she has more time. It could be you believe a certain task is not really your strong suit or at least not your cup of tea. How often do we think: That's a task beyond my skill and ability level. If I take it on, how can that possibly end well?"

Imagine I gave my eight-year-old son a hundred dollars and my car keys and told him to drive to the store and pick up some healthy snacks. I'm not sure I can count the ways that scenario could possibly go wrong. First of all, he doesn't know how to drive, other than in MarioKart. If he tried, he couldn't see over the dash. If he managed to operate the car, he wouldn't know the way to the store. Even if he somehow found his way to the store, he might, very possibly, lose the money before he got there. Once in the store, he might spend the money on something totally different than I had instructed him. And even if all the stars aligned and he made it to the store and purchased snacks, his idea of a healthy snack and mine are likely quite different.

Sometimes that's how I feel about being responsible for accomplishing God's work. Don't give me the car keys God! It's too much. It's beyond me. I'm not up to that challenge. The thing Gideon realized, and I often forget, is it's *God's* work. That's why He kept whittling down the size of the Israelite army. That's why their weapons were pottery and musical instruments. God wanted it to be clear to everyone that this was *His* plan – because no one else, in their right mind, would ever do it this way. He wanted it to be obvious the battle was won by *God's* power – because no one else had enough power to pull it off. He wanted there to be no doubt that this was *God's* victory.

Here's the thing, God could have defeated Midian without Gideon. If Gideon had said no, if Gideon had not answered the call, if Gideon had thought that trick with the fleece was just God's way of pulling the wool over his eyes, God could have still defeated Midian without Gideon. God could have found someone else to lead Israel. God could have done it without help from anyone if He had wanted to – POOF! a plague infects the Midianite camp and the entire army is wiped out. Yes, God could have defeated Midian without Gideon, but Gideon could have never defeated Midian without God.

HELLO
MY NAME IS
Deborah

Always Keep in Mind What is at Stake

Hello, my name is Deborah. I lived during the period of time after Moses and Joshua led Israel, but before Saul was anointed to be our nation's first king. During these years the country was led by judges – men and women who spoke for God and interpreted His law for His people. And it just so happens that I was selected by God to be one of those judges.

I've gotta tell you, I loved my job. My office was under the shade of a palm tree in the hills of Ephraim. People would come from all over Israel to have me settle their disputes and answer their questions. I went home every day feeling good because I knew I had helped people. I really liked that and if that had been my entire story I would have been content, but it wasn't.

Something happened that triggered a chain of events taking me from beneath my palm tree to in front of Israel's army. It all started when I received a message from the LORD. It didn't happen often, but when it did, it was usually pretty important. But before I tell you what the message was, there's something else you need to know first.

Prior to my time as a judge, things had not been going so well. The people of Israel had turned their hearts away from God. They started to do things God had told us not to do and they stopped doing the things God had instructed us to keep doing. This wasn't the first time and it wouldn't be the last. It seems we were rather easily swayed by the ideas and opinions of the nations around us who didn't worship the LORD.

Slowly and subtly we turned our backs on God and in an attempt to get our attention, He removed some of His protection from us. It didn't take long for a rival nation to take advantage of that. Recently, our biggest problems came from Jabin, king of Canaan. Jabin's army was led by a general named Sisera. The general was as cruel and ruthless as they come and he had the military to impose his will on whoever he wanted to. Often, it seemed, he wanted to impose it on us.

We lived under the boot of Sisera's army for many years, but gradually people started to turn their hearts back to the LORD and He heard our cries. That's when He sent me the message. God had chosen a man named Barak to raise an army and drive Sisera back across our borders. If you've ever heard the story of Gideon, I think God had something similar in mind. But that's not exactly how things turned out.

I sent a messenger to invite Barak to come from where he lived in the region of Naphtali and meet with me. When Barak showed up I don't think he knew what to expect, but I'm sure he wasn't expecting what he heard. I told him that God wanted him to raise an army of 10,000 men and go out to challenge Sisera.

"Sisera!" he said. "*The* Sisera? Are you nuts? You know he's got over 900 chariots, don't you? Nine hundred! And he has more infantry and archers than I can count."

"Yes, I know that," I replied. "But the LORD..."

"And even if I could recruit 10,000 men, which I highly doubt by the way," he interrupted. "What chance do farmers and merchants have against trained soldiers? No chance, that's what chance they have."

"I understand that," I explained. "But the LORD has promised to lure Sisera in and give him into your hands. And what the LORD has promised, He will do."

"I don't know," Barak said reluctantly. "On the one hand, I would like to trust God. But on the other hand, NINE HUNDRED CHARIOTS!"

"Go with the first hand," I suggested.

"Okay, I guess I'll do it...but on one condition."

"What is it?"

"You have to come with me," he insisted. "You're the one who told me to do this, so your fate will be the same as mine."

"Technically, God is the one who told you to do this," I reminded.

"You know what I mean. Besides, if you're with us, the LORD will be more likely to keep us safe."

"Fine," I conceded. "However, because you insisted that I come with you, the honor of this victory will not be yours – it will go to a woman instead."

Barak's face dropped. I could see the wheels turning and I knew exactly what he was thinking: It was bad enough that he had to go into a battle he was still pretty sure he was going to lose, but even if he did survive and somehow miraculously win, he wouldn't get any credit for it. Worse yet, all the glory would go to a woman. He had that same look on his face boys in elementary school get when they lose a race to a girl. Of course, at the time he thought the woman I was talking about was myself, but God had something else in mind.

Barak put out the call to the people of Naphtali and Zebulun and what do you know, 10,000 men volunteered to go out and face Sisera's army. We led the army to Mount Tabor and waited for God to draw out the Canaanites. It didn't take long for word to get back to Sisera and he mustered the full force of his army and marched them into the Kishon Valley. I told Barak the time was right. The men of Israel descended the mountain and attacked the army of King Jabin.

As Barak had expected, the battle was a completely lopsided rout. Contrary to Barak's expectations, we were on the winning side. The Canaanite army was crushed. Those who survived the initial battle fled. Sisera, himself, abandoned his chariot and scurried away from the battlefield on foot. Barak and his men chased down every last one of the enemy troops.

Sisera scrambled to find a safe place to hide out. I'm sure he was quite confused and distressed at this point. He had certainly not expected to get walloped by the men of Israel, I'm sure of that. He recalled that a man named Heber lived nearby. His clan had always gotten along well with King Jabin, but what Sisera didn't know was Heber had left his clan some time back. When he reached the tent, Heber's wife, Jael, was the only one home.

"Your people and mine are friends," Sisera stated. "I need a place to lie low for a while."

Jael invited the general in, offered him a soothing glass of warm milk, and then suggested he lay down and rest. Sisera agreed as he was utterly exhausted not only from the battle but also from being on the run. It didn't take long before he was sound asleep.

Before he had passed out, Sisera asked Jael to stand by the tent door and keep a lookout for any of the Israelites who were hunting him down. Jael stood at the front of the tent until she heard the general sawing logs inside. She went in and found him sleeping like a rock on a mat on the ground. Jael tiptoed around and picked up a long tent stake and a hammer. She silently knelt down beside the sleeping general, gently placed the tip of the stake on his temple and raised her hammer to strike.

Some time later Barak showed up at Heber's tent. He had been going from camp to camp looking for the general or any of the other Canaanite soldiers who were AWOL. Jael met Barak at the tent door and said, "I think I know what you're looking for." She ushered Barak into the tent where he found his enemy pegged to the ground.

I had told Barak a woman would get the credit for beating Sisera and I have to say, Jael really nailed it. More importantly, the LORD had kept His promise and the people of Israel enjoyed peace and prosperity for forty years following Sisera's defeat.

The story of Deborah is, in some ways, a tough one to process. Partly because it is not the story of one person, but rather the story of three or four people: Deborah, Barak, Jael and perhaps Sisera. It's hard to know exactly what to make of Jael's role in all of this, so we'll leave that analysis for far more wise and scholarly men and women to discuss. We don't know much about Sisera except he was the leader of a virtually unstoppable army that really enjoyed tormenting the Israelites for twenty years. That's a long time for any bully to pick on the same kid, which is likely why no one really feels bad when he meets his rather horrific demise. This leaves us with Deborah and Barak.

The second thing that makes this story tough to dissect is that I'm not sure it's really about what I've always been told it is about. I've always heard two things about this story. First, Deborah is an awesome, powerful, heroic woman. Second, Barak is a bit of a loser for doubting God when he is called to lead Israel against the Canaanites. The first is sort of true. The second may not be true at all.

Let's talk first about Deborah. Without a doubt, she was a special kind of woman. She is called both a judge, which could also be translated simply as leader or prophetess. These are not roles commonly held by women in the Old Testament, to say the least. Deborah is the only recorded female judge and one of a very few ladies named as a prophetess.

It cannot be denied that Deborah must have been a very special person to have been selected by God to serve in these roles for His people. Not because she was a woman, but because they are both sacred callings which the majority of people (male or female) do not receive.

It also goes without saying that it would have taken extraordinary amounts of courage and faith for any woman to take on such visible leadership roles in that time, place and culture. If you think there is a glass ceiling for women today, there was a glass floor in Deborah's time. Many others, no doubt, would have turned down the calling realizing that the hassles and resistance they would inevitably receive simply wouldn't be worth it. Deborah said "Yes," and, as it turned out, became widely respected, as witnessed by having a palm tree named after her and more importantly Barak's desire to have her accompany him into battle.

That being said, there is really nothing in the text to indicate Deborah did anything more than deliver God's message to Barak and then, at his request, accompany him to the battlefield. There is no mention or even indication, that Deborah fought in the battle, led the troops in any way or even gave a rousing "Win one for the Gipper" speech before the battle began. Some might infer from her statement declaring the glory for the victory would go to a woman was a reference to herself, but clearly, it was not. It was Jael who ultimately defeated Sisera and nowhere else do we read of Deborah being credited for the victory.

On the one hand, it is clear that Deborah's role shows God is just as eager to use women to accomplish His purposes in this world as He is to use men. It would seem that His primary concern is the ability to accomplish the task and even more importantly the willingness of a person to be used in whatever role God might call them to. Not only was Deborah a judge and prophetess, but she also delivered God's message to Barak and did whatever it took, including going to the battlefront herself, to ensure that God's mission saw its fruition. On the other hand, it is possible we've given her a little more credit than she would have given herself for the victory over Jabin's army.

Which brings us to Barak. I have always heard Barak's story pitched as the counter-point to Gideon. They both received a calling from God to raise up an army and free Israel from an oppressive force. They both were asked to face an enemy who was dramatically superior in size, skill, and weaponry. The difference is Gideon said, "Yes," and Barak said, "No."

However, I'm not sure that characterization is true or fair. After all, if you recall, Gideon didn't just jump on the bandwagon right away. Should we really label Barak the faithless doubter simply because he didn't think to test God with a liquid defying sheepskin – twice? Yes, Barak did ask God's appointed representative to go into battle with Him but don't forget, he did go, he did lead, he did fight and he did, undeniably with God's power, win. Sure, Jael was the one to finish off the leader of the Canaanite army, but at the time Barak was still tracking Sisera down, not being satisfied with simply routing the rest of the army, including those 900 iron chariots.

For those of you who are still having a hard time seeing Barak in the role of a faith-filled hero, consider the words of the writer of Hebrews:

> *And what more shall I say? I do not have time to tell about Gideon, Barak, Samson, Jephthah, David, Samuel and the prophets, who through faith conquered kingdoms, administered justice, and gained what was promised; who shut the mouths of lions, quenched the fury of the flames, and escaped the edge of the sword; whose weakness was turned to strength; and who became powerful in battle and routed foreign armies. (Hebrews 11:32-34 NIV, emphasis mine)*

That's pretty elite company for Barak to be keeping at the end of a chapter dedicated to men and women of great faith!

Perhaps one of the greatest lessons we can learn from this story is this: things aren't always as they seem. The spiritual giants and church leaders we know might not be exactly who we think they are. They may struggle more than we see. They may doubt more often than we expect. They may stumble more than we are aware. That's not to say they are not fit to lead; they just might be a little more human than we realize.

On the flip side of the coin, the lowlier among us may actually be accomplishing great things behind the scenes without anyone noticing. They may not get the credit for it, but their faithful service is a powerful tool in the work of the Kingdom. They may not hold position or title, but they press on quietly and accomplish the things God needs done.

The bottom line is God can and will use anyone who is willing to participate in His mission. Judges, prophetesses, generals, farmers, preachers, Sunday school teachers, cooks, cleaners, card writers, worship leaders, bulletin folders, greeters, food donators, and apparently, on some occasions, tent-peg-wielding house-wives. The question is: are you one of the willing?

I Did Not See That Coming

Hello, my name is Samson, and I should warn you, my story isn't exactly PG if you know what I mean.

Before I was even born, my parents dedicated me to God and committed me to the life of a Nazarite. For the record, a Nazarene is someone from the town of Nazareth. A Nazarite is someone who has taken a vow to be set apart for God – or in this case, someone whose parents took a vow for him.

The Nazarite vow has three basic principles.

1. You must never drink wine or vinegar or any other alcoholic beverage. In fact, he wasn't even supposed to eat grapes or grape seeds for fear of digesting one that was a little too ripe.
2. You must never get close to a dead body; you can't even be in the same room. Even if it is a close friend or relative you have to keep your distance so you don't get defiled.
3. You can never cut your hair. Some people were so strict they wouldn't even comb their hair because in

doing so they ran the risk of inadvertently pulling out a stand or two.

Anyway, fast forward about 20 years to when I was a strapping young lad, well built and full of muscles. My intimidating physique came from more than just working out. God had blessed me with extraordinary strength. One day I was traveling through the Philistine town of Timnah and came across this girl who was smokin' hot. I mean she was drop-dead gorgeous and I knew right then and there that she was 'the one!' I hurried home to tell my folks the good news, but you know how parents are.

They were all like, "Oi vey! A Philistine girl? Why can't you find a nice Jewish girl to settle down with, instead of a daughter of our mortal enemies?" But I didn't care what they said; my mind was made up. So, I went back to Timnah to meet this girl and make arrangements with her father to marry her.

While I was on the way, a young lion jumped out of the trees to attack me, but I just grabbed it and tore it apart with my bare hands like you would rip apart a young goat. What? Are you telling me that I'm the only one who used to tear apart goats? Hmm. Anyway, I tossed both halves of the dead lion into the bushes just off the road and continued on my way.

It wasn't long after when I was traveling the same road with my parents, this time headed for my wedding. I went ahead and, just out of curiosity, looked into the bushes to see if the lion was still there. Sure enough, it was, but it was buzzing with bees. They had made a hive inside the carcass. I reached in and pulled out a few honeycombs. I know I had taken a sacred vow to not get anywhere close to dead bodies, but I was really hungry and the honey just looked so sweet, I couldn't resist.

The wedding itself lasted for over a week. It was one big, long party. I was assigned thirty groomsmen to keep me company, occupied and out of trouble. I figured if I had to put up with these babysitters I might as well get something out of it. So, I told them, "I bet you can't solve my riddle before the end of the feast. If you do, I'll give you each a full set of clothes. But if you can't, each of you has to give me a full set of clothes."

They agreed so I told them this riddle:

From the eater came something to eat,

From the strong came something sweet.

For seven days, they guessed every answer they could think of, but none of them came close to solving it. That's when my bride came to me and said, "Honeybun, I don't think we're starting this marriage off on a very good foot if we keep secrets from each other. Do you?" I just grunted, which she took as affirmation. "So, I think you should tell me the answer to your silly little riddle. After all, if we can't trust each other, what hope do we have?"

What could I say to all that? I explained the riddle's solution to her and she said, "I love you, snookums," and then she returned to the party. Less than a minute later my groomsmen came in and, surprise surprise, they had the answer to the riddle! I was furious. I stormed out of the party. I marched thirty miles away to the Philistine town of Ashkelon and in my rage killed thirty men and stripped them of all their clothes. When I returned to Timnah I threw the clothes stolen from the dead men at my cheating attendants and said, "Here's your prize, now get out of my sight." Then I stormed out of the party again without a word and return to my home in Israel – alone.

A while later, after I had cooled off, I went back to Timnah to collect my wife. I figured I might need something to butter her up after I had made such a scene at the wedding. Nothing cliché like chocolates or flowers, no, I pulled out all the stops and brought a young goat. After all, if worse came to worse, I could always impress her by ripping it apart. However, when I arrived, her father met me at the gate and refused to let me in.

"When you stormed off like that, we figured you were gone for good," her father said. "We had the marriage annulled and she got married to one of the local boys instead." I think he could see me getting upset, so he offered, "But her younger sister is still single and I think she might even be better looking."

My blood was boiling. "Whatever happens next," I told him, "Just remember you asked for it."

It was right around harvest time, so I went out of the city and caught 300 foxes. I divided them into pairs and tied them together by the tail – which is no easy task let me tell you. I tied torches to their tails, lit them on fire and set them loose in all the fields and vineyards in the area. Burned them all to the ground.

Of course, the Philistines weren't happy about that so they went and burned down the house of my former father-in-law with his entire family inside. When I learned what they had done, I returned and shouted to the men of the city, "You should not have made me angry. You will not like me when I'm angry." I viciously attacked them all and killed a large number of them, before retreating back to Israel.

The Philistines raised an army of thousands and marched to Judah where I was hiding out. The leaders of the tribe of Judah came to me and asked what they should do. They didn't want to hand me over, but they didn't want to be invaded either. I told them to tie me up with two thick, strong ropes and leave me out in the field near the Philistine camp, so that's what they did.

When the Philistines saw me standing there, tied up and incapacitated, they rushed toward me to take me down. However, when they got close, God's power surged in me and the ropes became like paper streamers. I burst free and, wielding a donkey jawbone I found laying on the ground, I slaughtered a thousand Philistine soldiers before the rest ran away like scared little girls.

When it was all over I was totally worn out, so I cried out to God, "Did you help me become victorious in battle just to let me die of thirst?!" Just then, God split open a nearby rock and fresh cool water spilled out. I chugged back a bunch of it and felt much better.

Sometime later I was in Gaza, another one of the big Philistine cities. I was wandering the streets one night and saw a prostitute standing on the corner. I know that kind of thing is not pleasing to God, but on the other hand, she was looking mighty fine. She invited me back to her place and I eagerly accepted. The people of the city heard I was in town, after all, I had a bit of a reputation amongst the Philistines. They assembled all their troops at the city gate planning to ambush me when I left the next morning.

Luckily for me, I woke up in the middle of the night and decided to slink out of town. When I realized that they had laid a trap for me, I was furious. I charged the city gates and ripped them right off their hinges. I carried the huge wood and iron gates far from the city and set them up on the top of a hill facing Hebron. Removing the gates not only provided an escape route, but it left the city completely vulnerable to attack. Leaving the gates on the hilltop meant they had a long way to haul them back, but the gates were also like a giant billboard announcing to everyone around that the city was unprotected and vulnerable.

A while later I met a woman named Delilah. Yes, she was a Philistine as well, but, man, I'm telling you, on a scale of one to ten, Delilah was an eleven. I was instantly smitten with her and we started spending a lot of time together, if you know what I mean. What I didn't realize was the Philistine leaders had paid her off to find out the secret of my great strength. I just thought she loved me as much as I loved her.

One night, she said, “Sweety pumpkin, tell me why you’re so strong.”

I had to say something so I told her, “If I were tied up with seven bowstrings I would be just as strong as a regular guy.” That night, around 2 a.m., I woke up to Delilah shouting something about the Philistines attacking. Without thinking I jumped out of bed and chased the men out of the room. It wasn’t until after they were gone that I realized my hands had been tied with seven bowstrings which I had instinctively snapped when I woke up. Someone must have overheard our conversation I thought.

A couple of nights later Delilah said, “Sweety pumpkin, I’m glad you’re okay, but it appears you weren’t entirely truthful with me. What is the *real* secret to your great strength?”

I leaned in close and whispered, “If I were tied up with brand new ropes, I would be just as strong as any other man.” I woke up in the middle of the night again and found more Philistine attackers in my room. This time I noticed the two new ropes bound tightly around my wrists, but I snapped them with ease and chased the men away.

A few nights after that, Delilah said, “Sweety pumpkin, I’m kind of hurt that you lied to me twice now. Why won’t you tell me the secret of your great strength? Don't you trust me? Don't you love me?"

"Fine," I said. "But you have to promise not to tell anyone. If you weave seven braids of my hair into a fabric loom, pull it tight and secure it with a pin, I would be just as strong as any other man."

That night I woke up to shouts of "The Philistines are upon you!" I quickly realized that my hair was in seven braids that had been woven into a fabric loom and secured with a pin. At this point, it occurred to me that perhaps I sleep a little too heavily. Nonetheless, I got up and chased the men out of my house, yet again.

Delilah came up to me with pouty lips and puppy dog eyes and said, "Samson, seriously. Why do you hate me? Do you enjoy making me look stupid? I thought you loved me. How can you really love me if you can't even be honest with me? I just don't know if I can be with a man who treats me like that."

"I'm sorry baby," I pleaded. "I do love you. Tell me what I can do to make it up to you. You name it. Anything." As soon as I said the words, I regretted, but it was too late.

"Sweety pumpkin, what is the secret to your great strength?"

There was no way to get out of it now, so I told her, "I made a vow to God and since the day I was born my hair has never been cut. If my hair were cut, all my strength would be gone."

Well, you probably can guess what happened next. I woke up that night to find a dozen guys jumping me. I knew immediately something was wrong. They threw me to the floor and bound my hands. One of the Philistines rubbed the top of my bald head and said, "You're not so tough now, are you, hot shot?"

The Philistines gouged both my eyes out, bound me with bronze shackles and threw me in prison forcing me to push a grindstone round and round, day after day. That was a while ago now. Today Philistines are having a big feast for their god Dagon. There must be a couple thousand of people here. All the rulers and leaders are in attendance.

They've hauled me out to be put on display for people to laugh at. What they haven't considered is the fact that my hair has started to grow back. I asked the little boy who serves as my guide to position me near the two main support pillars of the temple. I know this is the end of the road for me, but I've asked God to fill me with His strength one last time so I can at least go out with a bang. The Philistines brought me out here for a show. Well, all I have to do is push these columns just a tiny bit more and the Philistines are going to witness a performance that is sure to bring down the house.

Have you ever sat down to watch a movie that you have seen several times before on TV? However, this time you are watching it on disc or streaming it. Not long into the film, you begin to realize: there's a lot of language and a couple of risqué scenes in here that I don't remember ever hearing or seeing before. Of course, the reason for this phenomenon is that TV stations who broadcast movies in prime time have to dub out certain words and cut certain scenes to make the broadcast appropriate for all viewing audiences. Discs and streaming services do not.

Samson's story feels a lot like that to me. When I read the account in the Bible, I realize, this is not the Sunday School story I grew up with. In that story Samson is a godly man, a judge even. He is a Nazarite, specially dedicated to God. He was super strong and his strength was a blessing from God because of Samson's goodness and faithfulness to his Nazarite vows. As a kid, I knew that Samson killed a bunch of evil Philistines with the jawbone of a donkey. But more than anything, this was a story of how the wicked Delilah seduces and tricks poor ol' Samson into giving up his secret and then ruthlessly betrays him. However, even after his eyes are gouged out, Samson remains faithful to God. As his hair comes back, so does his strength and in a last heroic act of self-sacrifice, he collapses the temple and takes out a bunch more of the good-for-nothing Philistines.

But that's not the story we read in Judges 14-16. Some of those elements are there, but they look a little different. There is also a whole bunch of stuff that got dubbed out somewhere along the way. Let's be honest: the dude was a mess. It's hard to read his story and not cringe more than you cheer. He was arrogant, selfish, foolish, easily lured in by women and with a fuse so short it could go off before it was fully lit. Just read through the story again and count how many people, and foxes were slaughtered by Samson, not on the field of battle, but in a cold-blooded fit of rage.

Samson's story defies logic. Sure, his super-human strength defies logic, but so does his monumentally bad decision making; his overwhelmingly poor choice in women; and his epically uncontrollable temper. Perhaps the most illogical part of Samson's story is *this* is the guy God selects to be judge and leader of His people! Are you kidding me? When we read this story in its entirety we discover Samson was not the humble sheriff in a white hat ridding the town of outlaws and other filthy varmints. No, he comes across a lot more like a womanizing street thug involved in an ongoing turf war with a rival gang.

I suppose you could make a case for Samson's story being evidence that God can use the most flawed person to accomplish His purposes in the world – which I have no doubt He does on a regular basis. Samson certainly fits that description. Nonetheless, it is difficult to see the life of Samson as anything other than a cautionary tale. This is what you should not do. This is how you should not act. This is who you should not be.

It is virtually impossible to read Samson's story in full and not come away with two sobering realizations. First, and most obviously, being unable to control your temper drives you into a series of ever-escalating negative situations. Watch the cycle of violence and anger spiral rapidly out of control:

- Samson is mad at his wife for spoiling his puzzle so he stomps off and leaves the wedding. Sure, he made a big scene, but no one got hurt, (unless you count those thirty random guys from Askelton).

- Samson comes back and discovers that his would-be wife is married to someone else, so he torches the fields and the foxes. Destruction of property? Sure. Cruelty to animals? Definitely. But so far, no human casualties
- The Philistines respond by killing the family of the girl Samson was supposed to marry.
- Samson retaliates to the killing of that one family by killing hundreds in that town.
- The Philistines raise an army to track Samson down. Samson bludgeons thousands of them to death.

That is a tremendous body count, all on account of one ruined riddle! And that's just in the first part of the story! Samson is an active volcano of anger ready to erupt at a moment's notice, or with no notice at all. And although most of us have never set fire to foxes or attacked people with a mule carcass, some of us can relate to Samson's short fuse a little more than we care to admit.

Of course, we typically don't commit multiple homicides; instead we choose more a subtle, but equally lethal approach to venting our anger. We storm out of the room. We cut others down behind their backs. We shout and yell in the hallways. We post scathing comments on social media. We push and shove in the parking lot. We key cars, throw pots, smash windows and punch walls. You're likely thinking "Yeah, but those aren't nearly as bad as what Samson did." I'd be inclined to agree with you if Jesus hadn't said:

> *"You have heard that it was said to the people long ago, 'Do not murder, and anyone who murders will be subject to judgment.' But I tell you that anyone who is angry with his brother will be subject to judgment. Again, anyone who says to his brother, 'Raca,' is answerable to the Sanhedrin. But anyone who says, 'You fool!' will be in danger of the fire of hell." (Matthew 5:21-22 NIV – emphasis mine)*

Jesus told His followers that anger comes from the same seed in our heart that murder grows out of. You have to root out that seed before it leads to bigger and badder things. James adds:

> *Understand this, my dear brothers and sisters: You must all be quick to listen, slow to speak, and slow to get angry. Human anger does not produce the righteousness God desires. (James 1:19-20 NLT – emphasis mine)*

And Paul writes:

> *"In your anger do not sin": Do not let the sun go down while you are still angry, and do not give the devil a foothold. ... Get rid of all bitterness, rage, and anger, brawling and slander, along with every form of malice. Be kind and compassionate to one another, forgiving each other, just as in Christ God forgave you. (Ephesians 4:26-27, 31-32 NIV)*

I think anger often gets brushed off as not a big deal. People say things like, "I have a quick temper. I've got a short fuse. That's just the way I am." But in God's mind, it *is* a big deal because it can quickly do a whole lot of damage to a whole lot of people. Samson never really figured that out, at least not until it was way too late. He never really got his anger under control and it ruined a big chunk of his life, not to mention causing immense pain and heartache to countless others.

The second, and rather obvious, realization is there are severe consequences from hanging out in the wrong places with the wrong people. Timnah, Askelton, Lehi, Gaza and the Valley of Sorek – virtually all the action in this story takes place within the borders of Philistia. I don't know if Samson spent the majority of his time in Philistine territory, but it's tough to deny that every time he did cross the line bad things happened.

What on earth was the guy charged with leading God's people doing spending so much of his time in enemy territory? It's not like he was there on a business trip. He wasn't there to tell the Philistines to back off and leave the Israelites alone. He was there for parties, prostitutes and marriage proposals.

I'm sure Samson didn't intend to get in trouble. He didn't mean to get sucked in. It wasn't his plan to be led off track. But Samson's life story is a blazing example of the reality: If you hang out with the wrong people, in the wrong place for too long, something wrong is bound to happen. And much like us, I'm sure Samson thought he could handle it. He was strong and tough. He knew better than to be led astray by the Philistines. Sure, they were evil, but they were also really fun to hang out with. If you asked Samson, I bet he'd say the same thing most of us say when we get ourselves into trouble: "I didn't think it would happen to me. I thought I had it under control. It just kind of snuck up on me."

I'll never forget something one of my college professors said to us in class one day. He was talking about a fairly well known, and often misapplied, verse in 1 Corinthians.

> *So, if you think you are standing firm, be careful that you don't fall! No temptation has seized you except what is common to man. And God is faithful; he will not let you be tempted beyond what you can bear. But when you are tempted, he will also provide a way out so that you can stand up under it. (1 Corinthians 10:12-13 NIV – emphasis mine)*

He said, "Sometimes the way out, is to not go in." Most of us wait until it's too late. We push it to the very last second and then say "Okay, God. I need a way out ... quick!" My professor said, "Sometimes we are like the alcoholic who walks into a bar, orders a drink and when it arrives begins frantically praying for God to provide a way out of the temptation to drink it. Perhaps the way out was to not go into the bar in the first place!"

Many times, like Samson, we get ourselves off track because we've been spending too much time with the wrong people in the wrong places. That's not to say you should move out to the middle of nowhere and cut off all communication with the rest of the world. You don't have to be a hermit in the woods. However, if you're regularly putting yourself in places and situations where temptation is abundant, if you are constantly hanging out with folks who, by their example or their encouragement, are prompting you to do things you know you shouldn't, I don't care how strong you think you are, it's only a matter of time before you start making mistakes you wish you could take back and crossing lines you never thought you'd cross. Just ask Samson.

HELLO
MY NAME IS
Ruth

Barley & Bunions

Hello, my name is Ruth. I still find it odd that people are interested in hearing my story. After all, I'm not famous or wealthy. I'm not royalty or a great warrior. I'm not a prophet, a priest or a judge. I'm not even an Israelite. I'm just a normal, every day, common woman from Moab. I was just a young girl, minding my own business, helping my parents weave blankets to sell at the market until one day everything changed.

I was minding the shop for my folks when a family I had never seen before walked in. It turned out they were new arrivals from Israel. Apparently, their land was experiencing a severe famine so Elimelech (Papa Eli as I would eventually grow to call him), had moved his wife and two sons to Moab. They needed some supplies to get their new home set up. Papa Eli told his eldest son, Mahlon, to stay and pick up some blankets while the rest of the family continued to shop the at the other booths in the market.

I was delighted for the opportunity, not only to sell a few blankets but more importantly to get to know Mahlon, who was, quite frankly, a dreamboat. He was young, handsome, strong, and, I have to say, a bit of a flirt. Mal started visiting our shop regularly. He would just hang out and chat while I wove. He was sweet and quite funny and it didn't take long for the seeds of love to blossom.

Sadly, it was not long after their family arrived in our village that Papa Eli became ill and passed away. The loss was extremely hard on all of them, but Naomi found comfort in the fact that she still had her two boys. She was overjoyed when Mal and I announced our engagement. Shortly thereafter, Mal's brother Kilion also married a Moabite girl named Orpah.

I left my parent's home and moved in with Mal and his mom. We were living on cloud nine. Mal was a great husband, so loving and kind. There were only two things that could have made life any better: if Mal's father had been there with us, and we had been blessed with children of our own. We tried all the old wive's tales and superstitious tricks, but nothing seemed to work. Every night in her prayers I would hear Naomi pray for grandchildren to carry on the family name, but it was just not meant to be. For whatever reason, neither Orpah or I were able to conceive.

Despite my bareness, we still had a wonderful, loving marriage. I remember as we celebrated our tenth anniversary I felt very content and I knew I could live happily with Mal even if we were never able to have kids. He was such a great guy. I was so happy. It was only a month or two later when both Mal and his brother, Kilion, came down with a strange illness. We did everything we could for them, but it was not long before they were both gone.

My world went into a tailspin. I felt like I was in some kind of altered reality. I remember walking around and muttering to myself over and over, “This can’t be real. This just can’t be real.” But unfortunately, it was. Naomi took her sons’ deaths really hard too. We tried to lean on each other for support, but we were both hurting so much we didn’t have much to offer each other.

Finally, a few weeks after the funerals, Naomi sat Orpah and me down and announced, “I’m going home. I’m going back to Israel. The famine is over and there is nothing for me here now. This land has taken everything from me.”

“Not everything,” I reassured her. “You still have us. You will always have us.”

“No,” Naomi stated firmly. “You girls are still young. Too young to spend the rest of your lives as grieving widows. You must stay here and find new husbands. Build new families.”

“You are our family,” Orpah declared.

“That’s sweet, but I will only be a burden to you. I will return to Israel and you lovely girls can go on with your lives.”

We discussed it for a long time, but it was clear that my mother-in-law would not be dissuaded. Eventually, Orpah conceded the argument and the two of them hugged one another and cried together. My sister-in-law left and returned to her own home. I stayed to help Naomi pack. However, once her belongings were all packed up, I started to pack my own things as well.

“Ruth, what on earth are you doing?” she asked.

“Wherever you go, I go. Wherever you live, I will live. Your people are my people and your God is now my God. End of conversation,” I stated resolutely.

“My sweet girl.”

The next morning, we loaded all of our things on a donkey cart, I kissed my parents goodbye and we began our journey back to Israel. It was very hard to leave them behind, but they had six other children to care for them in their golden years, Naomi had no one. We traveled to the city of Bethlehem in Judah, which is where Naomi and Papa Eli had lived prior to moving to Moab. Many years had passed, but the people still recognized Naomi and the town was abuzz with the news of her return. Very quickly reports spread about how there were only two of us and what had happened to Elimelech, Mahlon and Kilion – some true and some rather far-fetched.

I'd be lying if I said my pledge to stay with Naomi wasn't a little bit selfish. After all, the two of us had become quite close over the years. However, more than anything, I wanted to stay with her because the death of her sons had sent her reeling. When we returned to Bethlehem, she kept telling people that her name had been changed to Mara (which means bitterness) because she had lost everything. I refused to call her that, though. Even though she carried a great sadness, at the same time she held fast to her faith in God and the confidence that He would take care of us.

When we returned to Israel we had only a limited amount of supplies and very few means of supporting ourselves. It happened to be harvest time so I decided to go out to the fields and see if I could scrounge up some of the grain the harvesters missed. It likely wouldn't be much, but it might be enough to make a little bread. Naomi suggested I go to the field of a man named Boaz. He was a relative of Elimelech and might allow me to scavenge in his field if he knew I was Elimelech's daughter-in-law.

Sure enough, Boaz found me in his field and, once he knew who I was, he invited me to come back every day for as long as the harvest lasted. His generosity extended beyond that original offer. He also invited me to eat lunch with the hired workers and drink from their water jug. By the end of the first day, I had collected over 20 liters of grains! It wasn't until years later that Boaz confessed he had instructed his workers to purposefully leave extra grain behind when they saw me nearby. That's just the kind of guy he was.

Naomi was overjoyed to see how successful I had been at gleaning in Boaz's field. Little did I know the wheels were already turning in her head and she had started to play matchmaker. She told me to go back to his field every day because it would be safe and he would watch over me. But she also had something else in mind. Near the end of the harvest season, she gave me some special instructions.

"Come home from the field early today," she said. "Then put on your best dress, do up your hair and put on some fragrant perfume."

"What for?" I asked.

"When Boaz has finished his work and had his fill of food and drink he will fall asleep," she explained. "When that happens, you must sneak in quietly, remove the blanket from his feet and lay down."

"On his feet?" I asked, slightly grossed out.

Nonetheless, I did what Naomi told me. That night once Boaz had fallen soundly asleep I came into where he was laying. I uncovered his feet and laid down. In the middle of the night, he woke up and noticed me lying there.

"Who are you and what are you doing?" he asked in bewilderment.

It was the moment of truth. I repeated the words Naomi had given me. "I am your servant Ruth. Spread the corner of your garment over me." According to my mother-in-law, this was a subtle way of offering to be his bride. I waited anxiously for what seemed like forever. Eventually, Boaz spoke.

"I am flattered, to say the least. After all, I'm no spring chicken. There are plenty of guys younger and richer than I am, and believe me, you could have your pick of them. I would be honored to take you as my wife, however, according to our customs that privilege goes first to Elimelech's closest relative."

"Oh, I see," I said disappointedly.

"I will speak to him first thing in the morning. Go home and wait for my message."

I went home and reported everything to Naomi and then waited impatiently. Boaz, true to his word, went into town at first light and talked to Elimelech's closest relative. He told the man that he was first in line to purchase Elimelech's land, but with the land came the responsibility of caring for the dead man's widow and daughter-in-law. The man told Boaz that he did not have the means to purchase the land and care for the two women; therefore, the responsibility must pass to the next closest relative which just so happened to be Boaz.

"I will purchase the land of my relative Elimelech," Boaz declared in the presence of the town elders as witnesses.

"And I will care for his widow Naomi and take his daughter-in-law, the widow of Mahlon, as my wife."

The town elders blessed Boaz and it was not long before the wedding bells were ringing. Boaz took Naomi and me into his home and cared for us very well. He was an extremely kind man with a generous heart which made it easy to love him. Before long we had a child together and we named him Obed. In time Obed married and had a son of his own named Jesse. Jesse had eight boys, my great-grandsons. I was quite old by this time, but I still recall holding the youngest boy in my hands and thinking there was something special about him. His name was David. You may have heard of him.

I have to confess: When I initially wrote the first half of this chapter I was a little bit stumped about what to say here on the back nine. Of course, I was familiar with the story of Ruth and Naomi. I have heard it many times over starting with my earliest days in Sunday School as a child. As far as I can recall, virtually every time I have heard this story presented, the focus has always been on Ruth's unwavering dedication to Naomi and her refusal to let her mother-in-law return to Israel alone.

That is, without a doubt, a noble gesture. I'm sure we would all do well to emulate Ruth's loyalty and love. But, to be honest, I wasn't sure I could fill up the allotted pages ruminating on that point alone. Don't get me wrong, I love to write and I could easily fill up pages on just about any topic. I suppose what I should say is I didn't know if I could fill up the allotted space with words that were worth reading.

That was when I first wrote Ruth's story. As I come back to work on this chapter once again, a couple months down the road, I have a much different take on what is really going on here. You see, I am (hopefully) just coming off a couple of really lousy months.

I will not burden you with all the specifics but suffice to say our family went through a period of six to eight weeks where it was one thing after another on what felt like virtually a daily basis. We were hit with numerous serious health issues, extended family turmoil, extreme job stress and uncertainty, credit card fraud, unexpected major house and vehicle repairs and a variety of other high anxiety moments that pushed us right to the limits of what we thought we could handle: occasionally, a little bit beyond.

At this point in time, I can say the preachery thing and tell you that God carried us through it all and we were blessed terminal illness or death was not among the list. But there were times over the last couple months where I'm not so sure I could have said that, at least not with complete sincerity.

Which is why Ruth's story sounds different to me today. This is a tale tailor-made for all those who have been forced by life to adopt the motto, "Well, with my luck ...," or "What else could possibly go wrong?" It is a story that begins with famine and goes downhill from there. It is a journey marked at virtually every step by hurt, pain, and loss. It is for all those who look at their life and ask questions like, "How could this have possibly happened to me?" or "How on earth did I end up here?" And I'm old enough now to realize if you have never found yourself in that place, you probably just haven't lived long enough. Some of us get there sooner, or more frequently than others, but we all get there at some point.

What I like and simultaneously dislike about Ruth's story is that although she does eventually meet up with Boaz who takes her in and cares for Naomi as well, this is not the fairy-tale ending we hope for. There is no time traveling doctor from the future who shows up with a cure for Elimelech and a vaccine for Mahlon and Kilion. There is no erasing the pain of the past. There is no fixing the damage life has done. There is no escaping the pain. Even the apparent happy ending, as great as it is, does not leave us with a sense of full relief. We walk away feeling more like, "Well, at least there's that," rather than "I'm so glad it all worked out in the end."

At the end of the day, I think this story is less about Ruth's loyalty, Naomi's resilience or Boaz's generosity as it is about the inescapable reality that sometimes life stinks and really miserable, heartbreaking things happen, and yet, God does not abandon us. It is a reminder that the presences of bad does not indicate the absence of God. It is an assurance that just as Ruth walked with Naomi each step of the way, God walked with them both from start to end.

We live in a fallen broken world filled with fallen and broken people. People have free will and the ability to intentionally or unknowingly make choices that cause us hurt or pain. We live in physical bodies, in physical environments, both of which are susceptible to degradation. We exist in emotionally-charged situations and relationships prone to cause anxiety, stress, and heartache. You can run away from Israel to avoid the famine, but you might wind up in Moab with a terrible illness. You may find a husband, but be barren. You may stay with your mother-in-law but be separated from your parents. It is inescapable. It is life.

But the two truths that Ruth's story highlight for us are: God never abandons us and He always works to bring something good out of and into our lives regardless of what else is going on around us. Out of a story filled with tragedy, God brings joy into Ruth's life through Boaz. God brings children to the barren and an heir to carry on the line of Elimelech through Obed. He cares for two lonely widows through the generous heart of a kinsman. And you can be sure Ruth's grandson Jesse heard all about how God cared for and provided for her and Nana Naomi. How they trusted in Him and He came through. How, even in the worst of times, when everything seemed to be going wrong, God was still faithful. It was, no doubt, one of the many stories that shaped the young boy David into the man and king he would eventually become.

Ruth's story calls us to remember that when life's got you down, God's still got you. When things go bad, God is still working for good. And your faith and faithfulness in the hard times of life could very well turn out to be the very thing that inspires others to hold to their faith when their life gets tough too.

> *And we know that in all things God works for the good of those who love him, who have been called according to his purpose. (Romans 8:28 NIV)*

HELLO
MY NAME IS
David

A Tall Order

Hello, my name is David and this is my story. I grew up as a shepherd watching over my father's sheep in the pasture. It was a quiet peaceful life which I enjoyed very much – totally better than being at home with my seven brothers! With that many kids in the house it was always a bit of a zoo, but out in the fields, everything was calm.

I would spend all day wandering with the sheep or sitting under the shade of a tree. I loved to while away the hours playing worship songs on my harp. I even wrote a few of my own songs, believe it or not! When I wasn't playing my harp, I was taking target practice with my sling. I got pretty good at it too.

Of course, there was a lot of work involved with shepherding as well. The sheep were always wandering off or getting themselves stuck in a hole or rock crevice. They're not the brightest of animals, to say the least. And then, there are all the predators to worry about. Needless to say, it was in these moments that all my slingshot practice paid off. And let me tell you, nothing kickstarts your prayer life like staring into the eyes of an angry, wild beast. I recall one time where I had to fend off a lion without any weapons. The same thing happened again later on, except that time it was a bear that attacked the flock. I told my brothers I killed the beast with my "*bear*" hands, but they didn't find that nearly as funny as I did.

One day, one of my brothers came to call me in from the field. He said that the great prophet, Samuel, was at our house. I ran home to see what was going on. Sure enough, there was Samuel, sitting at our kitchen table. When I walked in, he stood up and poured oil on my head.

"You are the LORD's anointed one," he said.

I wasn't really sure what exactly he meant by that. Israel already had a king, our very first king as a matter of fact. Saul was tall, brave and very popular with the people at that time. I couldn't imagine how the crown could ever possibly pass to someone like me. For the most part I didn't worry about it much; instead, I just went right back out to the field to tend to my father's sheep.

Now, as I mentioned, it had not been long since we Israelites had appointed our very first king. It was also the first time we had ever had a standing army. Up until then, when a problem arose someone would put out the call for help from town to town. Whoever could go help in the battle showed up. But now, the new king and his new army had gone out to meet a large group of invaders. The Philistines were bigger, stronger, more numerous, better equipped and more skilled in battle than the Israelites.

The two armies meet at the Valley of Elah. The troops of Israel made camp at the top of the valley on one side and the Philistine army made camp at the top of the other side. This was the smart and safe way to do it. If an attack came, you could see it coming from a long way off. You also held the tactical advantage by defending the higher ground. What typically happened was eventually the two armies would converge down in the valley and duke it out, but not this time. This time was different.

For 40 days, the two armies stood and shouted at each other from across the valley. You see, the Philistines had a secret weapon: a giant, over nine feet tall! Twice each day, Goliath would come out and taunt the Israelites.

"Send out your best soldier," he bellowed. "We'll settle this mano a mano. If I win, all of you will be our slaves. If your man wins," he snickered and then said, "Let me try that again with a straight face. Ahem, if your man wins, we will be your slaves." It was a reasonable arrangement – especially if you know your guy is virtually guaranteed to win.

Naturally, no one in Israel was eager to jump at the opportunity. King Saul was arguably the best soldier in camp. He was no slouch either; in fact, at his coronation, he was recorded as being a head taller than everyone else there. Not to mention, being the king, he had the best armor and weapons too.

But Saul wasn't interested in facing Goliath. Instead, he offered a boatload of money and his daughter's hand in marriage to anyone who took on the giant – and won, of course. Not shockingly, there were no takers.

Twice a day Goliath came out and challenged the Israelites. When no one accepted his challenge, the giant would laugh at the army of Israel and mock their God.

That's when I showed up. Three of my seven older brothers were in the army and my dad sent me to the battlefront to check on them and bring up some fresh supplies; after all, they had been out there for 40 days.

When I arrived, everyone was just standing around. Then Goliath came out and did his usual shtick. The camp was dead quiet. I couldn't believe they'd let him get away with that. I couldn't believe no one shouted back. I couldn't believe no one went and put that overgrown loudmouth in his place. Fine, make fun of our army if you want – we know we're not what you'd call an intimidating force to be reckoned with. But if you have the gall to mock God, boy oh boy, you're going to get what's coming to you and I wouldn't want to be you when that happens.

I made my way through the crowd and walked up to the king's tent where Saul stood observing the taunts of the giant in the valley below. I told the king that I would go out to fight Goliath. My brothers told me to shut up and go home. At first, Saul tried to make me wear his armor, but it was so big, awkward and heavy I could hardly move. Don't forget, he was a big guy and at the time I was just a fifteen-year-old kid. To tell the truth, I don't think Saul wanted to send me out to fight the giant, but he wanted to do it himself even less. He knew the people were looking to him to do something soon because they were all tired of being camped on the battlefront, so, in the end, he agreed to let me go.

The only weapon I took with me was my handy-dandy shepherd's sling. When I reached the valley floor, I picked up a handful of stones from the creek bed. Don't be deceived, a sling looks pretty simple, but it can rifle a rock hundreds of yards at speeds of 60-80 miles per hour.

Goliath just laughed at me as I walked out to meet him. I literally thought he was going to fall over from laughing so hard. I have to admit, he looked a lot bigger face to face (more like face to waist) than he did from up on the hillside.

"Did you send a little kid to throw sticks at me?" he yelled up at King Saul.

I yelled back, "You might have a big and powerful sword, but I have a bigger and more powerful God." After all, I figured the guy deserved to know who he was up against and have a chance to change his mind and back out while there was still time.

Goliath just laughed some more. While the giant was busy being tickled by his presumed advantage, I started whipping my sling around. I could hear it whir as it circled above my head. Then, before he even knew what hit him, the stone shot through the air and nailed him right between the eyes.

The giant fell down and laid as dead as a corpse. Just to make sure the rest of his army knew it was over, I grabbed his oversized sword, hoisted it with two hands and chopped off his head.

At that point, all the Philistines freaked out and ran away. All the Israelites cheered and rushed across the valley to chase them down. Looking back on it now, I kind of feel bad for Goliath. Once he started calling out God, he never really stood a chance. He was totally out-matched; he just didn't know it.

The last time I preached this story at our church I created a life-size Goliath. At first, I thought it would be fun and cool. And it was. But what I was surprised at was how intimidating a two-dimensional Philistine could actually be. The peak of his helmet was about nine and a half feet from the floor. That sounds like a lot, but when I tell you that the man standing in front of Goliath in the photo is just an inch or two shy of six feet tall, it starts to sink in.

But there was more to it than just height. Sure, there are basketball players who are seven and a half feet tall – which by the way is still two feet short of this behemoth. But, Goliath was not built like Manute Bol. He would have been build more like our former youth minister who was also a competitive weightlifter. Goliath was big and strong. He was a career soldier and a champion warrior. The Bible actually notes his chest plate alone weighed 125 pounds. His spear was a daunting six feet long and the tip alone weighed 15 pounds. Which means these things were big enough and impressive enough that when the Israelites took them off Goliath's decapitated body they said, "Dude! These things are huge! We've got to weigh them and see how heavy they are!"

This battle is the epitome of a mismatch. The average height of an Israelite teen at this time was likely 5'2" to 5'3" (like the young man in this picture). Had David used a sword his blows would have landed closer to Goliath's knee cap than his shoulder.

When I was in college I had a group of friends, Kevin, Matt, John, and Kevin. One of the Kevins was just over six feet tall and he was the noticeably short one of the four. I was a towering five foot eight which meant every time we walked across campus together I felt like a junior high kid. Goliath was a professional soldier. David a shepherd. Goliath had weapons and armor. David had a strap of leather and a handful of rocks. The Philistines were shouting and high-fiving in anticipation of an overwhelming victory. The Israelites were cringing and looking in anticipation of a gruesome massacre.

It's easy to understand why so many people see this story as being about overcoming enormous odds. However, this is about something much more significant than just a little guy taking down a giant. The real heart of this story is about trust.

The Israelites' trust was in their weapons, strength and fighting skills – all of which were in far too sparse supply. They wanted to trust in their king, but more than anything they trusted the belief that none of them stood a chance against the mammoth man. King Saul's trust was in his own prowess as a warrior, his pretty tall for a Jew stature and the quality of his armor. The Philistine army trusted in their giant, their champion, their guaranteed win – which seemed like a sure thing right until the moment he fell to the ground, dead. Goliath trusted in his strength, his size, his skill, his shield, his spear and his sword.

And here's the thing: All of those seemed to make perfect sense in the moment, didn't they? If you had been standing in the Israelite ranks, looking across the valley at the Philistine army, what odds would you have given yourself? If you had been King Saul looking down at the monstrous man mocking your monarchy, how confident would you have been? If you had been one of the Philistines who had seen Goliath completely annihilate any and all who dared to challenge him, without breaking a sweat, wouldn't you be feeling pretty good about your chances? If you were nine feet tall and full of muscles who would you be remotely scared of in any physical contest?

For 40 days everyone in that valley saw things exactly the same way. The Philistines were heavy favorites. The Israelites were huge underdogs. Goliath was too big, too strong and too powerful. No one could challenge him, let alone defeat him. No one was crazy enough to go up against him, no matter how great a reward King Saul offered. The oddsmakers would have let you wager as much money as you wanted to on anyone defeating the giant because everyone saw it as a sure thing.

Well, almost everyone. David came along and he saw things differently. He saw the Philistines as already defeated. He saw Goliath as a guy without a chance. He saw Israel's victory as inevitable, a foregone conclusion really. In other words, he saw the situation from God's perspective. But he didn't just show up on the battlefield that day and decide "I think I'll look at things from God's perspective today." No, David had been developing and honing his ability to see things from God's perspective every day of his life. He had become so accustomed to viewing life through the eyes of God in everyday, ordinary situations that when he came to this extraordinary situation it was just natural for him to see it that same way.

David's trust was not in his speed to outmaneuver the giant or his lethal aim with a slingshot. His confidence did not come from his ability to kill a lion or a bear in search of a free mutton meal. David's trust was in one thing alone. Listen to him say it for himself:

> *David said to the Philistine, "You come against me with sword and spear and javelin, but I come against you in the name of the LORD Almighty, the God of the armies of Israel, whom you have defied. This day the LORD will hand you over to me, and I'll strike you down and cut off your head. Today I will give the carcasses of the Philistine army to the birds of the air and the beasts of the earth, and the whole world will know that there is a God in Israel. All those gathered here will know that it is not by sword or spear that the LORD saves; for the*

> *battle is the LORD's, and he will give all of you into our hands." (1 Samuel 17:45-47 NIV – emphasis mine)*

This story is a reminder that God is calling his people to trust Him. even when the odds seem against it; Even when logic seems to defy it; even when our gut objects to it, God says "Trust me. I've got this." It won't always be easy. It won't always be not scary. And there is no guarantee that we will always slay the giants in our lives, but God's promise is: Whatever you face, whatever challenges are in front of you, however things are going and however things turn out, trust Me, we'll get through this thing together.

There is one other lesson to be gleaned from this fantastic story that is often missed. I confess it had never occurred to me in all dozens or perhaps hundreds of times I had heard this story until recently. Consider this: The battle was at a stalemate for 40 days. For 40 days, the two armies shouted across the valley at each other. For 40 days, Goliath taunted them, morning and evening. For 40 days, King Saul offered ever-increasing rewards to anyone who could defeat the giant. For 40 days, everyone in Israel said, "Thanks, but no thanks."

And yet, for 40 days, God was ready willing and able to take Goliath down, to defeat the enemy and to win the victory. All He was waiting for was one willing volunteer. It could have been King Saul. It could have been one of David's three brothers. It could have been *anyone* in Israel. This whole thing could have been over on day one, if someone, anyone, had stepped up and said, "My trust is in the LORD. I'm looking at the situation through God's eyes."

Which makes me wonder. How many situations in my life have dragged on because I failed to trust in God? How many opportunities have I missed because I failed to see things from God's perspective? How many times has God been waiting for someone like me to step up and say, "I'm willing … You're able. You lead … I'll follow. With You beside me, I can face whatever is in front of me."

> *Be strong and courageous. Do not be afraid or terrified because of them, for the LORD your God goes with you; he will never leave you nor forsake you." (Deuteronomy 31:6 NIV)*

HELLO
MY NAME IS
Jonah

A Whale of a Tale

Hello, my name is Jonah and I am a prophet of the LORD, although, I have to admit, that was not my first choice. God selected me and as much as I tried to say, "Thanks, but no thanks," God was not taking no for an answer.

My story begins several years ago when the LORD spoke to me for the first time. There I was, minding my own business, just hanging out in my hometown of Joppa when God called to me.

"Jonah," He said, "I have a job for you."

At first, I was quite excited, honored even. I mean, not everyone gets a personal assignment from God, right? But my enthusiasm quickly evaporated when I found out exactly what it was He wanted me to do.

"Jonah, I want you to go to Nineveh."

"Nineveh? Nineveh! Are you kidding me? Why on earth would I want to go there? Why would *anyone* ever want to go there?"

"You will tell them if they do not repent I will destroy their city."

"Humf. Nineveh, you'll never find a more rotten den of filth and delinquency," I muttered to myself. "I've got a much better idea God, why don't we just skip the whole preaching thing and just wipe those slime-balls off the face of the earth right now!"

I know that sounds harsh, but you've got to understand, the Ninevites were really bad dudes. They were cruel, heartless and sadistic. What do you expect from a city founded by a guy named Nimrod? – true story.

Nineveh was the capital city of the Assyrian Empire. The Assyrian army was powerful and they were known for laying siege to defenseless cities. Once the gates had been breached they would slaughter everyone – men, women, children, everyone. Almost everyone in Israel had friends or family that had fallen to an Assyrian sword.

If you asked me, wiping Nineveh off the map would be good news for everyone. I suppose you might expect me to be excited to deliver God's message to the Ninevites; after all, it did carry the threat of obliteration, which was a stellar idea in my books. However, it carried something else too: a call to repentance. And you know how God is: He will literally forgive anyone who genuinely repents.

Even though I thought the odds of getting through to the stone-hearted Ninevites was ridiculously low, I didn't want to take that chance. Even if there was a one in a million chance the Ninevites would hear my message and repent, I knew that if they did, God would forgive them. And I didn't want to be the guy who got them off the hook. I certainly didn't want the people in Israel to know I was the guy who got them off the hook. Not to mention, the Ninevites likely wouldn't take too kindly to some foreigner coming in and telling them they are evil sinners and they must all repent or some god, who they don't even know, will wipe them out. That's a proclamation I didn't expect to live long enough to fully deliver.

What was I to do? I gave it some thought and came up with what I thought was a brilliant idea at the time. "They can't ever respond to God's message of repentance if no one ever delivers the message," I reasoned. So, I packed a bag and went down to the harbor. I booked passage on the ship going the farthest distance in the exact opposite direction of Nineveh. In this case, a cargo ship headed to Tarshish on the western coast of the Mediterranean.

I walked on board and slunk down into the hull of the ship. I wasn't interested in chit-chat or anyone asking too many questions about where I was headed and why. As far as I was concerned, if I didn't speak to another soul until we reached Tarshish, that would be A-Okay with me.

It wasn't long into our voyage when a violent storm came up one night. I was sleeping so soundly the pitch and lean of the ship didn't wake me, nor did the reverberating claps of thunder. One of the crewmen eventually found me and shook me awake.

"The ship is about to go down, this is no time to be sleeping!" he screamed.

Frankly, I figured if the boat was going to sink, I'd prefer to sleep through it than have to suffer through the terrifying ordeal wide awake, but now, thanks to the panicking crewman, that ship had sailed. So, I went up to the deck to see exactly how bad things were. When I got there, I saw crew members frantically tossing cargo overboard. I knew things must be serious because that was their income and reputation going into the drink. They wouldn't do that unless they felt it was the only way to survive the storm.

However, even these desperate measures would not be enough. The storm continued to get worse and eventually I heard the captain shout out, "Whatever god you pray to, now is the time!" That didn't sound good at all. Not long after, the captain gathered me and some of the other men together and said, "The gods must be angry with someone on this boat. We must find out who it is so we can appease the god's wrath."

We cast lots to see who the guilty party was and guess who drew the short straw? You guessed it. I can't say I was terribly surprised. I explained to the men that God was angry with me for sailing to Tarshish instead of going to Nineveh as He had instructed.

I told the men to throw me overboard, but instead, they tried to turn the ship around and sail back to Joppa. I guess they figured once they got me moving in the right direction, God would be satisfied. But God cared about more than geography. My heart still wasn't in His mission. The storm continued to get worse and finally, the men agreed to toss me over the deck rails. To tell the truth, I was just as happy. At that point, I still would have rather drown in the sea than have to go back and preach repentance to Nineveh.

As soon as I hit the water, the wind died down, the sky cleared and the sea went calm. The men on the boat were in awe of the power of God. I was bobbing in the water wondering what came next. I didn't have to wonder long. Before I knew what was happening, I was swallowed whole by a giant sea creature. I slid down its throat and landed with a splash in the darkness and stench of its belly.

I know lots of people have debated whether it was a fish or whale or a cousin of the Loch Ness Monster, but let me tell you from firsthand experience, from the inside, none of that really matters. To be honest, I don't know what was more frightening: to be swallowed alive, or to be stranded in pitch black darkness of its stomach.

At this point, there was only one thing left for me to do – pray. And that's what I did. For three days, I prayed to God. Then, without warning, the fish's stomach convulsed and I was propelled back up the throat and out of its mouth. I landed in the water, just offshore. I turned around just in time to see my former accommodations splash and dive back under the surface of the water.

I did my best to clean myself up, but my skin was bleached a ghostly pale color from the gastric acid and no matter how many times I washed it, I could never get that fishy smell out of my hair.

Once I had somewhat pulled myself together I traveled to Nineveh and preached the message God had given me to the people. Much to my surprise – and I admit, great dismay – the people received God's message and took it to heart. Everyone from the king on down repented of all their cruelty and evil ways. As promised, God forgave the Ninevites and spared them from destruction.

If I'm being honest, I'd have to say the way it all played out was a little tough for me to swallow, but then again, I imagine that's what the fish thought too.

Perhaps the clearest and most inarguable truth found in the story of Jonah is this: You can run, but you can't hide from God.

When Jonah decides to decline God's directive, he does his level best to get as far away as he can, as fast as he can. I assume he thought if he made it to Tarshish he could escape

God's notice, or at the very least he would be too far away from Nineveh to be of any use.

To fully appreciate what's going on here you need to take a look at a map.

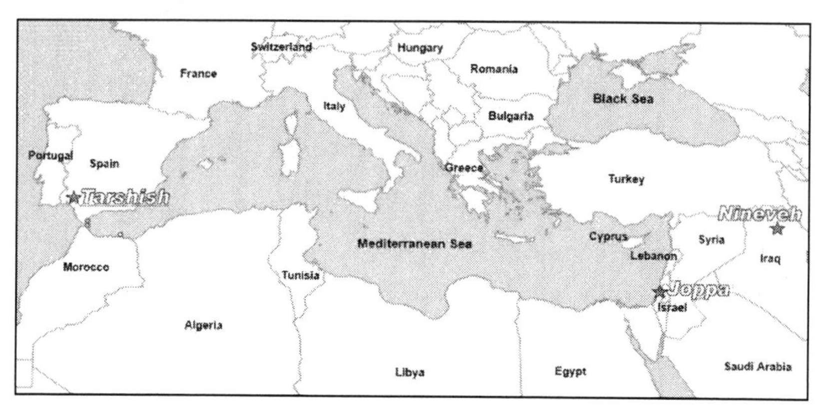

Jonah was in Joppa when God called him. God wanted him to take a short little hike up to Nineveh, however, Jonah bought a ticket on a boat sailing for Tarshish instead. Tarshish is on the west end of the Mediterranean Sea, through the Strait of Gibraltar, in what is today southern Spain. This was literally believed to be the ends of the earth in Jonah's day. The only thing, as far as they knew, farther to the west was a whole lot of ocean until you reached the great abyss at the edge of the earth. Had Jonah's boat kept sailing due west after Tarshish the next stop was Virginia Beach.

But no matter where Jonah went, God was there. Perhaps he should have read the words of Psalm 139 before he bought his ticket.

> *Where can I go from your Spirit? Where can I flee from your presence? If I go up to the heavens, you are there; if I make my bed in the depths, you are there. If I rise on the wings of the dawn, if I settle on the far side of the sea, even there your hand will guide me, your right hand will hold me fast. If I say, "Surely the darkness will hide me and the light become night around me," even the darkness will not be dark to you; the night will shine like the day, for darkness is as light to you. (Psalm 139:7-12 NIV)*

No matter where you go, God is there with you. Not in a creepy stalker kind of way. Not in a watching your every move so that as soon as you mess up, He can jump out of a bush and say, "Ha! Gotcha!" Think of it more in a caring parent kind of way. I remember when my kids were little. I would drop them off at school and sit in the car for a moment. I would watch them walk to the school door and go inside, before I drove away, just to make sure they made it okay and they didn't need anything else before I left. That's how God watches over you,

No matter where you're at, no matter what's going on, no matter what's happening in your heart, no matter how far from God you may have run, no matter what storm you are currently trying to weather, God is there with you. In fact, you couldn't get away from Him if you tried.

If Jonah's experience isn't enough to convince, consider the Ninevites. By all historical accounts, they were a mean, nasty, cruel-hearted, evil-doing people. There is no indication in the story they were seeking God. No suggestion they had called out to God. No reason to infer they had any knowledge of or interest in God before Jonah arrived in their city. And yet, God sends His prophet to them to try and reach their hearts.

What is more shocking is that within a single generation the Assyrians invade Israel. They conquer God's people and oppress them for nearly a century and a half until the Assyrians eventually gave way to the Babylonian Empire, which is the geopolitical equivalent of out of the frying pan – into the fire as far as the Israelites are concerned. But, even knowing their repentance will be short-lived, God sends His prophet to call the people of Nineveh back to Him. As the Apostle Peter declares:

> *Then Peter replied, "I see very clearly that God shows no favoritism. In every nation he accepts those who fear him and do what is right.* (Acts 10:34-35 NLT)

Paul also states:

> *This righteousness from God comes through faith in Jesus Christ to all who believe. There is no difference, for all have sinned and fall short of the glory of God, and are justified freely by his grace through the redemption that came by Christ Jesus.* (Romans 3:22-24 NIV)

No matter who you are or where you are at, no one is too far gone for God to reach out to them. God simply refuses to give up on people. He refuses to abandon them.

Have you ever wondered why God didn't just let Jonah sail off into the sunset? He could have, right? Surely there was someone else who could have delivered the message to Ninevah. There must have been others in Israel who could have been commissioned to call the Assyrians to repentance. For that matter, if God gave the message to Jonah, why couldn't He just give the message directly to the king of Nineveh? So that can't be the reason God pursues Jonah

I'll confess, I think part of me has always assumed the storm and the whole getting swallowed by a fish thing was somehow God's way of punishing Jonah for disobeying His instructions. I'm pretty sure that was the subtext of more than one Sunday School class: Don't disobey God or a whale will eat you! But I don't think so anymore. I think Jonah getting gulped by a giant guppy was about redemption, not punishment.

Imagine what would have happened if God had just let Jonah go. Jonah would have traveled to Tarshish in a foreign and pagan land. He would have been exiled from his home, his family and the temple. His relationship with God would be shattered, and he would spend the rest of his life convinced that his only hope was to stay off God's radar. Instead, God goes to great lengths to get Jonah's attention, to get Jonah turned around and headed back in the right direction, to transform him from a spiritual runaway to a powerful prophet.

So, unless you've run off to the ends of the earth to hide from God in willful disobedience to what you know He has called you to do and be, or even if you have, God is always right there with you. God is constantly reaching out to you. God is desperately trying to get your attention. God is earnestly calling you back into relationship with Him.

HELLO
MY NAME IS
Elijah

Fire and Brimstone

Hello, my name is Elijah, and I am a prophet of the LORD. I grew up in Gilead on the eastern shores of the Jordan River. You may have heard of it; the region is quite famous for its medicinal cream, which led to the coining of the phrase: Gilead, it's the balm.

When I became a man, God began to use me to deliver His messages to the people of Israel. Most of my messages were addressed to one guy in particular: King Ahab. King Ahab was inarguably the worst king Israel had ever had. God once told me that Ahab had done more to provoke Him than all the kings of Israel before him – which is saying a lot because there were some real duds in there as far as honoring God is concerned.

Ahab was bad enough on his own, but then he married this Phoenician woman named Jezebel and things went from bad to worse. She was so wicked that no parent dared name their daughter Jezebel for the next 3000 years. King Ahab, under the influence of the queen, promoted the worship of other gods throughout the nation of Israel. He even built a temple for the god Baal with an altar and an enormous Asherah pole. There were a few of us who remained faithful to the LORD, but not many.

Finally, God had had enough. He sent me to the king with this message: "Starting right now, there will be no rain upon the land. Crops will wither, creeks and rivers will dry up. There will be a drought and famine across all of Israel." It broke God's heart to see His people suffer like this, but He was desperate to find a way to get their attention and nothing else had seemed to work.

From that day on, not a drop of rain fell on the land. King Ahab was furious. He sent men off in every direction trying to track me down, but they never found me. These men threatened everyone they met, but no one knew where I was. Ironically, I was staying with a widow and her son in the town of Zarephath. The funny thing is, Zarephath is in Phoenicia, Queen Jezebel's home country of all places! While I was there, God made sure that all three of us stayed well fed and healthy.

After three years, when the land of Israel was drier than a slice of matza bread, I returned to the king. When he saw me, Ahab scoffed, "Is that you, you big troublemaker?"

I looked him right in the eye and declared, "The LORD says, 'Enough is enough!' It's time to settle this once and for all. Meet me on top of Mount Carmel. Bring the 450 prophets of Baal and the 400 prophets of Asherah. Be sure to invite all the people to come witness the event as well."

A couple days later we all met on top of Mount Carmel at dawn. There was a huge turnout, including all 850 prophets and the king himself. I announced to the people, "This will be a trial by fire. We will both build an altar and call out to our gods. You will call out to Baal. I will call out to the LORD. The true God will send fire to light the sacrifice on the altar. The false god will do nothing." Everyone agreed to the terms of the challenge. "Just to show you I'm a gentleman, I'll let you guys go first."

The prophets of Baal feverishly built their altar and prepared a bull to go on top of it. Then they started wailing and bellowing to Baal to send fire. They kept it up all morning long. You really have to admire their tenacity if nothing else. Around noon, as I sat in the shade eating some hummus it seemed like the prophets of Baal were losing steam, so I decided to *encourage* them a bit.

"Don't give up now! I'm sure your god is going to respond any second. Perhaps he's daydreaming or maybe it's his nap time.

You might need to shout louder to wake him up. Or maybe he's in the little Baal's Room and can't hear you. Which reminds me, did anyone check his calendar? I sure hope he's not on vacation this week!"

They were not nearly as amused as I was. They doubled their efforts to get Baal's attention. They sang, danced and shouted. Some of them even started cutting themselves with knives and swords, which I really didn't understand, but you certainly couldn't question their conviction. They kept it up all afternoon, but as sunset approached, I felt sorry for them and decided to put an end to their misery.

"Good try guys," I said. "You look exhausted and a little anemic. Why don't you take a breather and let me give it a shot for a bit?"

The prophets of Baal agreed and collapsed from the fatigue. I rebuilt the altar of the LORD that used to stand on Mount Carmel but had long since fallen into disrepair. I added some wood on top and then prepared the bull for the sacrifice. I wanted to make it clear, once and for all, that the LORD was the true and only God. So, I dug a trench around the altar and I told some men to fill four large jars with water and pour them over the altar. Then, I had them do it two more times just to be safe. The bull, the wood, and the altar were all dripping wet and the trench in the ground was overflowing with water.

I knelt down near the altar, but not too close, and prayed, “LORD, reveal to this people that you are GOD, the true God and that you are giving these people another chance at repentance.”

No sooner had the prayer left my lips than everyone gasped “Goodness, gracious!” A great ball of fire came streaming down out of the sky. The fireball landed directly on the LORD’s altar. The blaze was so intense it incinerated not only the bull and the wood but the stones as well. It scorched the ground and evaporated every drop of water in the trench.

Everyone was astounded and they all fell face first to the ground. They shouted, “The LORD is God!” over and over again. I instructed the people to take the prophets of Baal into custody and not let a single one of them escape.

Then I glanced out over the sea. I turned to King Ahab and said, “I hope you brought an umbrella. It looks like rain to me.” That night the LORD blessed the people with a great rain and put an end to the drought that had been upon the land.

At the start of the day King Ahab thought he was pretty hot stuff, but he quickly learned: if you can't take the heat, get off the mountain.

As is true with many of these stories, to really appreciate what is happening here, you have to have an appropriate sense of scale. In this case, you have to feel the heat. Elijah didn't light his sacrifice with a match or one of those fire sticks you use to start your barbeque. This is not some nice little campfire fire that you let die down to embers and coals so you can roast marshmallows. This is a nobody-walks-away-with-eyebrows kind of fire! Just in case you think I was embellishing a bit when I retold the story a minute ago, let me read it to you straight from the Bible.

> *Then the fire of the LORD fell and burned up the sacrifice, the wood, the stones and the soil, and also licked up the water in the trench. (1 Kings 18:38 NIV)*

I remember as a kid, a visiting preacher told us about the time he tried to recreate the story of Elijah on Mount Carmel at a camp. He piled wood in the campfire pit and constructed a zipline from the top of a nearby building down into the pit. The plan was to attach a torch to the zip line and when Elijah prayed, send the torch sailing down into the pile of wood. Of course, he wanted to make sure the wood caught on fire, so he added some gasoline to it. Apparently, he added too much. When the time came, the flame flew down into the fire pit and BOOOM! As I recall, the shock wave of the blast blew out the windows in the mess hall. I remember thinking at the time, "Cool! I want to go to *that* camp!" Now, that may be a little bit of overkill as far as the camp insurance broker is concerned, but it's probably just about right for this story.

God is not being timid here. He's not slipping notes in class so the teacher doesn't notice. God is making a statement to His people: You want to trust in the god of rain (aka Baal)? Fine, you won't see another drop until *I* say so. You want to put your faith in the god of lightning (also Baal)? Here you go, one flaming bolt coming up. BOOM! Drop the mic and walk away.

God is sending a message to His people and in the end, they finally get it. The message is clear: The LORD is God. This is a universal truth. Nothing we think, say or do will ever alter this reality. We might forget it, we might deny it, but in the end, when the smoke clears (literally in this case), the LORD is God.

There is a reason God demonstrates His presence so definitively here. The reason is revealed in Elijah's prayer:

> *Answer me, O LORD, answer me, so these people will know that you, O LORD, are God, and that you are turning their hearts back again." (1 Kings 18:37 NIV)*

Did you catch it? Elijah asks God to show up so the people will know the LORD is God, and that He is turning their hearts back again. All of this:

- The drought
- The challenge
- The giant fireball

All of it was for one purpose and to one end: not for God to show off, not for God to flex His divine muscles, not for God to prove He was better than Baal, not for God to intimidate people into believing in Him. This was all about reminding the people that God was God so they would turn their hearts back to Him.

This is not a case of my god can beat up your god. From God's perspective, this isn't a head to head cage match between Him and Baal. This is a rescue mission! This is God doing whatever He can, whatever He has to, to get His people's attention and say, "Hey guys, I'm over here! Please come home."

And for a moment, on Mount Carmel, the message got through. Baal was exposed, God was revealed. The people remembered God. They turned their hearts back to God. They renewed their relationship with God. For a moment.

That's what the whole battle was about. Everyone is gathered on top of Mount Carmel and...

> *Elijah went before the people and said, "How long will you waver between two opinions? If the LORD is God, follow him; but if Baal is God, follow him." But the people said nothing. (1 Kings 18:21 NIV)*

Elijah says, pick a side. Make up your mind. Quit flip-flopping back and forth based on what is popular or convenient at the moment.

If you think back to the story of Gideon, you will remember that one of the first things God had Gideon do was destroy the altars to Baal and tear down the Asherah poles. Back in the days of Gideon, the Israelites were seduced by the hip, trendy gods of the Canaanites.

That may not be surprising to you, but what you need to know is that Gideon (1191 BCE) and Elijah (860 BCE) lived over 300 years apart. Which is why Elijah says, "How long are you going to keep this up?"

I love the simplicity of Elijah's challenge to the people. He says, "Hey, if Baal is the true god then, by all means, stick with him. But if the LORD is God – follow Him." He is basically telling the people if the LORD isn't really God, then fine, ignore Him. Disregard His instructions. Don't bother worshipping Him or offering sacrifices to Him. But if the LORD *is* God, then, for crying out loud, live like it. Follow His instructions consistently. Devote your heart to worshipping Him. Do what he calls you to do.

This is very similar to what Joshua had told the people more than five hundred years earlier as the Israelites first entered the land of Canaan.

> *"Now fear the` LORD and serve him with all faithfulness. Throw away the gods your forefathers worshiped beyond the River and in Egypt, and serve the LORD. But if serving the LORD seems undesirable to you, then choose for yourselves this day whom you will serve, whether the gods your forefathers served beyond the River, or the gods of the Amorites, in whose land you are living. But as for me and my household, we will serve the LORD." (Joshua 24:14-15 NIV)*

Both Elijah and Joshua are challenging God's people: If you believe God is who He says He is, then get out there and live like it. Be who God wants you to be. Make the choices God wants you to make. Say the words God wants you to say. Forgive those God wants you to forgive, (which is everyone). Love those God wants you to love, (also everyone). Care for those God wants you to care for. Serve where God wants you to serve. Prioritize what God wants you to prioritize.

If you are reading this book and thinking, I'm not convinced that I believe in the God of the Bible. I'm glad you're still reading. I'm glad you're pondering those questions. Keep searching and God will lead you to the answers you're looking for.

For those readers who have already decided this is what is true; this is what is right; this is what is real; this is what is best for my life, this story is a reminder and a challenge to live out that belief.

It's easy to criticize the Israelites and be mystified by their habitual rejection of God, but, if we're honest with ourselves, most of us don't do a whole lot better. We all get distracted. We all get swayed by those around us. We all wander off on our own pursuing other sources of knowledge and contentment. And when we do, God does the same thing with us as He did on Mount Carmel. Hopefully, it won't take a drought or an explosion to get our attention. No matter how He does it, the message is always the same: turn your heart back to God. Renew your relationship with Him. Then go live it out each and every day.

HELLO
MY NAME IS
Naboth

Not For Sale

Hello, my name is Naboth. No, not Nabob – that's the coffee guy. *My* name is Naboth.

Don't feel bad if you don't recognize my name. I'm not that famous. I am not a king or prophet. I am not a warrior or a miracle worker. I am a viticulturist, which is just a fancy way of saying, "I'm a lowly grape farmer." In fact, I'm not even the main character in my own story! I likely come in third, or perhaps a close fourth.

The real star of this story is King Ahab. He was mean, selfish and cruel. He also couldn't have cared less about what anyone else thought, including God. He was a real piece of work, that guy, but nothing compared to his wife Jezebel.

One day, King Ahab was strolling around on one of the palace balconies when something caught his eye: my vineyard. The palace grounds were extensive, not to mention lush and well groomed, but something about my vineyard enamored the king.

So, there I was, working away in my vineyard fertilizing my grapevines when I heard footsteps approaching from behind me. I turned to find two of the king's personal guards standing there, looking very stern.

"The king wants to speak with you," they informed me.

"Oh, okay," I stammered. "Alright, um, just let me get myself cleaned up a bit."

"Now," they insisted. I followed them out of the vineyard where I found the king and several more guards waiting. With a little assistance from a guard behind me, I knelt down before the king. He extended his ring-laden hand to me.

"Oh, but, my..." I tried to explain, showing my filthy hands to the guard.

"Ha-ha," the king chuckled in a way that only someone pretending to laugh at something they don't actually think is funny can do. "A little bit of dirt won't kill me."

I took the king's hand in my grimy paws and kissed it. Of course, I neglected to mention that I had been fertilizing and it was not dirt they were covered in. "What brings your majesty to my humble home?" I inquired.

"Nathan," the king began.

"Um, it's Naboth, your highness."

"Ah yes, Naboth. I saw your vineyard from my palace balcony and I said to myself, I've just got to have it."

"I'm sorry, my lord, it's not for sale. Doesn't the king already have many vineyards of his own?"

"Oh yes, of course. I have plenty of vineyards. Most of them produce grapes far superior to this peasant variety. No, I intend to plow the whole thing under and use it for a vegetable garden or something. Be reasonable now; you haven't even heard my offer."

"It doesn't matter," I explained. "This vineyard has been in my family for many generations. I've put my whole life into grooming these vines. I wouldn't sell it for any price."

"You drive a hard bargain, Nicolas," the king interjected. "Very well, name your price."

"I wasn't negotiating, your majesty," I explained. "It's not for sale. Period."

The king turned around in a huff and stormed out of my yard. One of the guards knocked me over on his way out just for good measure. The king returned to his palace, went to his chambers, slammed the heavy oak doors and collapsed in a heap on his bed. Rumor is that he stayed there for days. He couldn't sleep. He wouldn't eat. He was in such a foul mood that no one dared enter the room. Eventually, Queen Jezebel came to check on him.

"What are you doing in here?" she asked. "You've been pouting and sulking for days. What has got you so upset?"

"Norman won't sell me his vineyard!" he exclaimed.

"What? You mean Naboth?" the queen replied. "He's a nobody. You're the king for goodness sake. If you want something, you take it – whether they like it or not. If you want Naboth's vineyard I can get it for you. Just leave to me. Now, man up and get out of bed."

Jezebel sent letters to the leaders of my town and signed King Ahab's name to them. The letters instructed the noblemen to have a feast and invite me as the guest of honor. What I didn't know at the time was that they had hired a couple scumbags to set me up.

Right in the middle of the feast, these stooges stood up and start making all sorts of outlandish claims about how I had blasphemed God and cursed the king. Normally, no one would have believed them, but because Jezebel had already instructed the nobles about what to do, and no doubt threatened them with what would happen if they didn't, I was doomed from the outset.

I was dragged out of the feast and taken to the edge of town. Everyone picked up rocks and started throwing them at me. They kept throwing until I was dead.

Obviously, I got the rest of the story second hand, but here's what I'm told happened next. When King Ahab heard what had happened, he immediately seized all of my property and belongings as assets of the state. This included, of course, my family's vineyard.

When King Ahab returned to the palace after having watched all of my precious grapevines get rototilled under, he was met with, what was for him, a very unpleasant surprise. The prophet Elijah was there waiting for him.

"You have been up to your usual wicked tricks," Elijah accused. "God has seen what you have done to Naboth and you will pay the price for such treachery. God has told me that your kingdom will be taken away from you."

"But it wasn't my fault," Ahab said trying to weasel out of it. "Jezebel's the one who set it all up."

"God knows that," Elijah replied. "And because of it, she will die a horrible death."

At that point, Ahab genuinely repented and turned to God for mercy. God allowed Ahab to live out his years, but when his son took over as king, he was almost immediately invaded, deposed and killed. As part of the coup, Queen Jezebel was thrown from her bedroom window in the palace, trampled by horses and devoured by dogs. Not a very pretty end to her story, I know, but, then again, neither was the end of mine.

This story is all wrong, and I don't like it.

It is all wrong because Naboth is a decent guy. He's just trying to make a living growing grapes on his ancestor's land. He refuses to sell his vineyard, and according to Levitical law, the king wasn't allowed to purchase land given as an inheritance anyway. And what does he get for doing the right thing? His family name is dragged through the mud, his vineyard is unlawfully seized and he is brutally murdered. I don't like that.

It is all wrong because King Ahab is a jerk. He's a guy who's already got more than he'll ever need, and most of what he could possibly want. And yet, he sees Naboth's little patch of land and decides he just has to have it. When he doesn't get his way, the king throws a hissy-fit and spends days pouting in his royal chamber. In the end, he gets exactly what he wanted, Naboth's vineyard. And when Elijah shows up to call him on the carpet, he repents and seems to get off virtually scot-free. I don't like that.

It is all wrong because Jezebel goes after Naboth for no other reason than to get her mopey husband to call off his pity party. She sets Naboth up, extorts people to lie about him, then ensures he is convicted and executed despite his innocence. She does, eventually, get what's coming to her, but it wasn't for more than a decade. In the meantime, she continued to rule the roost as she saw fit. I don't like that.

It is all wrong because it comes a mere three chapters after Elijah bested the prophets of Baal and Asherah on top of Mount Carmel. Three chapters after the people of Israel had supposedly turned their hearts back to God. Three chapters after God had ended the drought. Three chapters after the prophets of Baal and Asherah were executed for leading the people of Israel astray. Three chapters after crummy King Ahab had been sent scurrying home with his tail between his legs.

That was supposed to be the happy ending. That was supposed to right the ship, to bring justice to the kingdom, to restore balance to the force. It was supposed to be the turning point of the story. Things were supposed to be back on track after Mount Carmel, but instead, here is what happens:

> *Now Ahab told Jezebel everything Elijah had done and how he had killed all the prophets with the sword. So Jezebel sent a messenger to Elijah to say, "May the gods deal with me, be it ever so severely, if by this time tomorrow I do not make your life like that of one of them." Elijah was afraid and ran for his life. When he came to Beersheba in Judah, he left his servant there, while he himself went a day's journey into the desert. He came to a broom tree, sat down under it and prayed that he might die. "I have had enough, LORD," he said. "Take my life; I am no better than my ancestors." (1 Kings 19:1-4 NIV)*

And so, when we get to Naboth's story, Ahab and Jezebel are still running the show. God's law is twisted and manipulated to have an innocent man killed. And God's people not only stand by and let it happen, they are willing co-conspirators. I don't like that.

Nothing in this story seems right. Nothing turns out the way it should. Nothing goes how I'd like it to. So, what do we do with that? I'll be honest, part of me thought, "The easy answer is: don't include this troublesome tale in your book." Pick some other story instead where everyone is happy and things all work out the way they're supposed to. That certainly would have solved the problem from one standpoint. However, it was too late. I had already written the first half of this chapter, which meant, even if I cut the story from this book, I would still have to wrestle with those questions myself. So, we might as well wade through this together.

Most of the stories in the Bible reveal one of two things: the goodness of God or the corruption of the world. Naboth's story is one of the latter. The events of 1 Kings 21 teach us one thing clearly: life is not always fair. Things don't always go your way. Bad things happen to good people and other people often get rewarded for their bad behavior. Naboth's story underscores the truth that sometimes doing the right thing doesn't go well. The only people who can't relate to that are those who haven't done the right thing very often. Those who make a practice of doing the right thing, know all too well that many times doing right ends wrong.

Naboth's story ends all wrong. It's one of those stories you have to reread to make sure you understood it properly the first time. What kind of a Bible story is this? The guy does what he's supposed to, but ends up being publicly humiliated, branded as a blasphemer and a traitor, and killed in an intentionally dishonorable way. That doesn't seem right, does it? No, it doesn't. No, it's not. But, yes, sometimes life is like that.

Just ask an infant born with a life-long handicap, ask the ten-year-old who is diagnosed with diabetes, the twenty-year-old diagnosed with epilepsy or the thirty-year-old hit by a drunk driver. Ask the forty-year-old single parent, the fifty-year-old who just got downsized at work, the sixty-year-old with no pension, or the seventy-year-old with Alzheimer's. Ask the non-smoker with cancer, the parents who've lost a child, the kids who have lived through their parent's divorce, the spouse who has been cheated on or the senior citizen who has been swindled out of their meager life savings by some fast-talking investment salesman.

As much as we may not like Naboth's story, most of us can relate to it. Life's not always fair. I wish it was, but it's not. Even for Christians, life in a corrupt world doesn't always turn out the way it should. It didn't for Naboth. It hasn't for me. It likely won't for you.

The story of Naboth is included in the Bible not only to underscore the complete wickedness of Ahab and Jezebel, which it does very well, but also to remind us about the world we live in. Even more importantly, it's there to assure us that God is not oblivious. He sees what is happening around us. He cares what happens to us.

I have known far too many people who have struggled or completely given up on their faith because their life didn't go the way they wanted it to. People who have desperately wrestled with questions like, *"If there is a God, how could He let this happen?"* or *"If God really loves me, why doesn't He do something?"* If you have asked those questions yourself, please understand, I'm not making light of the hurts and challenges you've had to deal with. I know some of them. They are real. They are big. Some of them are really big, bigger than anything I've had to face thus far. So, please don't get me wrong, I'm not saying, "We've all got our problems, so suck it up, buttercup."

However, from time to time, we need to be reminded that the unfairness of life is not evidence of the absence or apathy of God. The unfairness of life is evidence of a world that is contrary to God's design and desire.

There was a time when life was fair, when everything turned out the way it should, when things always went right. And then, God allowed us to make our own choices. From that time on, fairness was no longer a constant. People were negatively impacted by their own actions and the actions of others. Our world began to decay and suffer the effects of its own corruption.

Yet, even in our defiance, God is still there. Even amidst our brokenness, God is still working. Even in the middle of undeniably rotten times, God still cares for us.

God understands the plight of all the Naboths among us. If you ever find yourself questioning this truth, let me remind you of a familiar story:

> Once upon a time, there was a man who always did the right thing. He was a man who always did what God wanted to be done. And yet, he was turned upon by those designated by God to be His representatives in Israel. He was falsely accused and convicted. He was publicly humiliated. He was branded a blasphemer. He was executed in a most dishonorable way.

You might be thinking I just recapped Naboth's story from a few pages ago, but I was actually talking about someone else.

The paragraph above is a description of Jesus. When God came to earth and dwelt among us, this was His experience. When God walked the earth, life was unfair, evil prospered, bad things happened to good people, enemies attacked, friends betrayed and things didn't turn out the way they were supposed to.

God gets it. He understands. He has been in your shoes. And He promises to walk with you each step of the way, through the good times and bad, when things go right and when things go wrong, when your plans work out and when they fall through, when your vineyard produces a bumper crop and when the Ahabs and Jezebels of this world conspire against you. God is with you. His heart breaks for you. His strength will see you through.

> *The LORD himself goes before you and will be with you; he will never leave you or forsake you. Do not be afraid; do not be discouraged.* (Deuteronomy 31:8 NIV)

HELLO
MY NAME IS

Elisha

It's No Small Thing

Hello, my name is Elisha. I was a prophet in Israel. Of course, when most people hear my name, they typically assume that someone has simply mispronounced Elijah. Elijah was a great prophet as well and my mentor for many years. When he recruited me, he said that I must carry on his work after he was gone. I assumed he meant in several years after he had grown old and died. However, much to my surprise, neither of those two things happened. One day we went off alone together. All of a sudden, out of nowhere, a flaming chariot swooped down out of the sky, grabbed up Elijah and flew back into the heavens.

I was declared Elijah's successor by the other men of God in the land. I continued on from where he had left off, but our work looked quite different at times. Elijah had spent much of his lifetime going head to head with the kings of Israel who refused to acknowledge the Lord as their God. My efforts were much more low-key.

I recall on one occasion where a woman came to me shortly after her husband had passed away. She was utterly distraught, not only because she had lost her spouse, but she owed some men money and her creditors were about to sell her two sons into slavery to recoup the money she owed. She told me the only thing she had of any value was a small amount of oil.

"Here's what I want you to do," I told the widow. "Go home and ask all your neighbors if you can borrow whatever empty jars they have on hand. Collect as many jars as you possibly can."

"What good are empty jars if I have nothing to put in them?" she asked.

"Bring all the jars into your house, close the door and begin to fill them with the oil you have."

"But how will ..."

"Just trust me," I assured.

The woman did as I instructed and gathered a large number of jars in her house. She began to fill them with the little bit of oil she had on hand. Much to her surprise, she had enough oil to fill the entire first jar. She continued filling the second and third jars as well. On and on she went until every jar in the house was brimming full of oil. When all the jars were finally full, the last drop of oil flowed out of her pitcher.

The widow took the jars back to their owners who paid her for all the oil they were now filled with. She collected enough money to not only pay off her creditors in full but to also ensure that she and her two sons would have enough to live off of for a long time to come.

On another occasion, a wealthy couple fixed up their guest room and offered it to me as a place to stay whenever I was in town. I was very grateful to have somewhere to lay my head, so I asked what I might do for them in return. The woman had, for a long time, desperately wanted to have children of her own, but had never been blessed with that joy.

"By this time next year," I pronounced, "You will be holding your own child in your arms."

I don't know if she really believed me at first, but it wasn't long before she was convinced. Sure enough, just as I had foretold, in less than a year's time, the couple had a son.

Several years later I was up on Mount Carmel, worshipping at the altar my predecessor had constructed when I saw this same woman rushing toward me. She was visibly upset, so I asked her what was wrong.

"My son was out in the field working with his father," she explained. "He came home complaining of a severe headache. We did what we could for him, and yet he only got worse and worse. We tried everything, but ..."

She broke down into heart-wrenching sobs. The servant who was with her explained that the boy had died from his illness. The woman was so utterly distraught. It had been painfully difficult for her to not have a child for so many years, but that grief was nothing compared to the anguish of losing her young boy. I simply could not stand to watch her suffer, so I return with her to her home. I found the dead boy lying on my bed in the guestroom. I went into the room alone and prayed. The Lord heard my prayer and the boy opened his eyes, once again full of life.

Then there was the time when the commander of the king of Aram came knocking on my door. His name was Naaman and he was, by all accounts, a good man. Unfortunately for him, he had contracted leprosy, which was in my day an incurable disease. Leprosy was also deemed to be highly contagious and thus all those whom it infected were shunned from society.

Naaman's wife had a young servant girl who happened to be a Jew. The servant told him that if he came to Israel, I could heal him. Needless to say, he was more than a little bit skeptical, but he was also incredibly desperate, so he came to Israel to find me. When he arrived at my doorstep, I sent my servant out with a message.

"The man of God says you should go to the river Jordan and dip yourself down into the water seven times. If you do this, you will be healed." You might think Naaman would be pleased to hear the solution was so simple. He was not. In fact, he was furious.

"How insulting!" he ranted. "I've come all this way to find him and this *man of God* can't even be bothered to come to the door and deliver the message himself! And what kind of treatment is this? Washing in the Jordan River? Gross me out! The Jordan is like sewer water compared to the clear, clean rivers we have back home! Forget this, I'm leaving."

That would have been the end of it too, but some of the men traveling with Naaman pursued him to reconsider. They argued if I had asked him to do something great and lofty he would not have hesitated, but because my instructions were simple he was disgruntled. After all, they reasoned, who cares what the treatment involves as long as it works. And work it did. Naaman went down to the Jordan and washed himself in the water repeatedly. When he came up out of the water the seventh time, he was completely healed and there was no trace of leprosy left on his body.

Ironically, it was not long after when the king of Aram made war against Israel. However, he did not have much success because, whenever he planned an invasion, I would tell the king of Israel exactly when, where and how the attack would come. Every time the Arameans made their move, Israel was one step ahead of them. The king of Aram became furious, convinced that there must be a spy amongst his inner circle. One of his officers explained that it was me, not a spy, that was perpetually throwing a monkey wrench into his battle plans.

The king sent out a battalion of chariots, horses, and men to track me down and take care of me, once and for all. The soldiers arrived in the middle of the night and surrounded my home. When my servant looked out in the morning, he began to freak out. He was convinced that we were utterly doomed and this was the end.

"Don't be afraid," I comforted him. "We are not the ones who are badly outnumbered, they are."

"What are you talking about?" he asked. "Have you seen how many soldiers are out there?"

I prayed to the Lord and asked God to open my servant's eyes so he could see what I saw. I told him to look outside again. He looked again and saw the hills and surrounding area were filled with horses and chariots of fire belonging to the army of the Lord.

The Arameans attacked and I prayed again. This time, the Lord struck every last one of them blind on the spot. I went out and spoke with the battalion commander. I told him they were in the wrong place and offered to lead them where they needed to go. He agreed and the entire army followed me as I led them right to the king of Israel.

Needless to say, the Arameans were more than a little surprised when I opened their eyes again. The king asked if he should slaughter them all, but I told him not to lay a hand on any one of them. Instead, I told him to hold a great feast and give the soldiers all the food and drink they wanted. The king followed my instructions and then sent the men back to Aram, unharmed, and from that day on the Arameans stopped invading our territory. I guess you could say they finally saw the light.

I feel bad for George Lazenby. If you don't know who George Lazenby is, you're likely not alone. If you do know who George Lazenby is, it's likely not in a good way. Lazenby's claim to fame, or notoriety, is that he is one of the handful of men to take on the role of Ian Fleming's James Bond, secret agent 007. Initially, that sounds like a good thing. What an honor to be part of a film franchise that spans more than five decades and, to date, 24 films (25 if you count Never Say Never). So, why is Lazenby's name so infamous?

The Bond franchise started out in 1962 with the film Dr. No, starring the young hunk Sean Connery. Connery is considered by many to be one of, if not the best to ever play the part, which would make him a very tough act to follow. After his fifth film, Connery left the role and the studio brought in Lazenby to take over the role of England's most charming spy. Unfortunately, George's portrayal of the iconic character, not to mention the script he was given, were so dismally lack-luster that, not only was he fired after completing only a single movie, but the studio begged Connery to return to salvage the franchise.

I wonder if that's how Elisha felt sometimes. After all, he was left with some pretty big shoes to fill. His mentor, Elijah, was and still is considered to be one of the greatest, if not the greatest, prophet Israel has ever had.

Think back to the mount of transfiguration. This is the moment when Jesus cracks the door of heaven and gives Peter, James, and John a brief glimpse of His true nature. And who is it that shows up on this momentous occasion? Moses, who was viewed by the Jews as the giver of the Law, and Elijah. Not Isaiah, not King David, not Father Abraham, but Elijah.

And when Jesus asked His disciples what the word on the street was about who He really was, they told Him Elijah was one of the top vote-getters, right up there with John the Baptist. Matthew includes Jeremiah further down the list, but Mark and Luke simply say, "one of the other prophets." Elisha was in the "other" category.

Imagine having to follow Elijah's act, having to live up to Elijah's reputation, having to live in Elijah's shadow. Elijah was the man who went toe to toe with Ahab and Jezebel. Elijah was the man who caused and ended nation-wide multi-year droughts. Elijah was the man who took on 850 prophets of Baal and Asherah at once. Elijah was the man who called down fire from heaven hot enough to incinerate stone. How would you like to be next in line after him?

Elisha's stories are, on the surface, much less impressive. More often than not he interacts with individuals, not large groups. He talks with commoners, not kings. There's only one time where it appears things might really start to amp up when a squad of Aramean soldiers and chariots have surrounded his home. The hillside is filled with flaming chariots of the army of God. Alright! It's showtime! Something big is about to happen, right? Not so much. There is no great battle; instead, Elisha leads the temporarily blind soldiers to the king where they are given their fill of food and drink, not to mention their eyesight back, and sent home without a scratch, a threat or an ultimatum.

Believe it or not, the stories I included in the first half of this chapter are the highlights. I skipped over the time when Elisha made an ax head float or made poisoned stew edible by adding flour. I didn't mention that he once fed 100 men with 20 loaves of bread or, my personal favorite, called a bear out of the woods to attack some bratty kids who called him baldy. I even omitted the story about the city that was held under siege for a long time and then, one day, the attackers just decided to go home.

However, even though the stories of Elisha may not have the scale and pizzazz of his predecessor, they are not without value. In fact, Elisha's stories show us something that we don't really see in the Elijah years: God's care for people. Not His care for nations or kingdoms, but His care for individuals. Elisha doesn't often deal with huge conflicts and great battles; he spends most of his time addressing the needs of ordinary, everyday folks like you and me: a widow who can't pay the bills, a couple who can't get pregnant, a parent who has lost a child, a man with a terrible illness. These are not international incidents or global crisis. This is real life people stuff.

Time and time again, God, through His servant Elisha, demonstrates His care and concern for one man, one woman, one family. God reveals His heart for people who are hurting. God shows His empathy for the oppressed. The stories of Elisha are stories of people who realize when they have nowhere else to turn, God is standing right beside them. He is not insensitive to their pain. He is not oblivious to their suffering. He is not indifferent to their needs.

Even the story about the Aramean army showcases God's tender heart for people. These guys had been actively raiding and attacking Israel. They had come to Dothan specifically to take out God's spokesman. He had them surrounded with chariots of fire and angelic forces. It would not have taken much to obliterate them on the spot – both sending a clear message to the king of Aram and decimating his military forces. But, instead of wiping them out, He ends up throwing a party for them and sending them home with gift baskets.

God is not hiding in bushes and peaking around corners trying to catch you doing something wrong so He can crush you. He is not scrutinizing your life with a fine-tooth comb looking for some reason, any reason, to really let you have it. The stories of Elisha show us that God is searching for a way to help. He is longing for a chance to heal. He is looking for an opportunity to fix what is broken and lift up what is fallen.

This grace is not just for His people in the broad sense or humanity as a whole, but for individuals. It is for me; it is for you; it is for each one of us. It is for the lonely, the oppressed, the hungry, the abused, the downtrodden, the hopeless, the worn out, the barren, the grieving, the sick, the unemployed, the estranged, the addicted, the broken-familied, the terminally ill, the disabled, the disadvantaged, the insecure, the lost, the overwhelmed, and the wounded.

The stories of Elisha may not have the glitz and fanfare that some other stories have. They may not have the size or scale that other events have, but their impact on the individuals involved is larger than life.

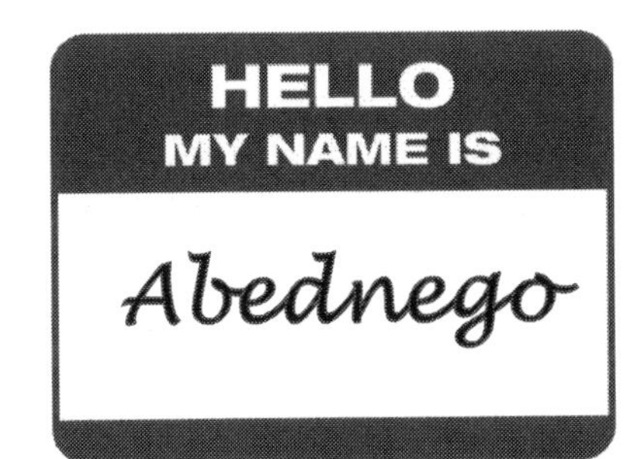

A Hot Mess

Hello, my name is Azariah and these are my friends Hananiah and Mishael.

If none of that sounds familiar, it's probably because you know us by our Babylonian names: Shadrach, Meshach, and Abednego. You may be wondering why we each have two different names. Well, it's not just us. Our buddy Daniel, whom you may have also heard of, was often called Belteshazzar.

You see, when we were all around 10 to 15 years old, our homeland of Israel was invaded and conquered by the Babylonian Empire. The Babylonians took a whole whack of us Israelites and exiled us to foreign lands. Some were sent to other nations in the Empire. Some of us were taken to Babylon itself. In return, the Babylonians put some of their own people and exiles from other conquered nations in Israel. It was all part of their "Defense Against Revolution" policy.

Once in Babylon, the king took the best and the brightest of our people. He educated us and gave us government jobs. He also gave us new Babylonian names. The theory was that this would encourage us to assimilate into Babylonian culture and thus be less likely to rebel and cause trouble for the Empire. It also ensured that the king always had the very best and smartest people working for him, not against him. Of course, there were some of the native Babylonians who weren't really happy with this plan, especially when guys like us advanced higher and faster than they did. Some of them really hated taking orders from a foreigner, but you should ask our buddy Daniel all about that.

Anyway, fast forward about ten years when one day, out of the blue, we received a memo saying we were supposed to go out to the plains of Dura with a bunch of the other rulers, advisors, and officials. When we arrived, we found ourselves in front of a 90-foot-tall golden statue.

We heard someone making an announcement, "When the band starts to play, everyone must bow down and worship the golden statue the mighty king, Nebuchadnezzar, has made."

Of course, despite being exiled from our homeland, the three of us continued to faithfully worship the LORD our God. We knew our God would not want us to worship this oversized idol. What were we going to do? We talked it over and we all agreed that no matter what happened, we would not bow.

The moment of truth came. The band played their music. Everyone around us began to bow. Now, we're not super tall guys by any means, but when everyone around you is on their knees you stand out no matter how vertically challenged you might be.

Just to make sure our upright posture did not go unnoticed, some of our Babylonian colleagues shouted out to the guards, "Hey, look! Over here! The Jews aren't bowing!"

The soldiers waded through the prostrated crowd. They grabbed all three of us and dragged us in front of the king. He told us he would give us a second chance, but then he made us an offer he thought we couldn't refuse: bow down and worship the statue or be thrown into the fiery furnace.

The music played. We did not bow. The king was furious. The soldiers dragged us off to the furnace.

We tried to brace ourselves for the agony that we knew was about to come, but the king was fuming mad. Just incinerating us would not be enough to pacify him. He instructed the guards to stoke the fire to seven times its normal temperature.

The king said, "I'll give you one last chance."

But we told him, "God can save us from the fire, but even if He doesn't, we won't worship anyone but Him."

That was the last straw. Nebuchadnezzar had all three of us bound by his strongest men and then they pushed us forward until we fell into the furnace.

I won't lie, I was a little bit terrified at this point. I believed God could rescue us, I just figured if He did it would be *before* we went into the fire. I was wrong. I felt the searing heat all around me as the guards launched my body into the flames. I hit the furnace floor with a thud. It may sound strange, but I remember the first thing I noticed was the ropes on my hands and feet had been incinerated. Then it dawned on me: I'm not dead. I should be, but I'm not.

I heard Hananiah and Mishael calling out, not in pain, but more like bewilderment. We eventually managed to find each other amidst the flames and stood together for a moment, not really knowing what to do or say at that point. Suddenly there was someone else standing with us. It was tough to make out his face, but I'm convinced it was God. Suddenly a feeling of peace swept over me, right there, in the middle of the blazing furnace.

After a while, Hananiah said, "I think they're calling us to come out."

He didn't have to tell me twice. As the three of us climbed out of the furnace together, we saw the bodies of the guards who had thrown us in laying on the ground – slain by the intense heat of the flames. When we got out, we looked at each other and were astonished to see no burns. Not a single hair was singed. We didn't even smell like smoke!

The king stared at us with a glazed look in his eyes. With a trembling voice, he declared, "I decree that no one is permitted to ever say anything against the God of Shadrach, Meshach, and Abednego." And then, get this, he gave all three of us a big promotion!

Before we get into this story, there's something you need to know. Nebuchadnezzar didn't just randomly build a statue. A while before this story takes place, the Babylonian king had a dream and it freaked him right out. He called a bunch of his advisors and asked them to interpret the dream for him. There was one proviso, the advisors had to tell the king what the dream was first, *then* explain what it meant. How else would Nebuchadnezzar know if these guys really knew what they were talking about or if they were just making stuff up and waxing elephants?

Not surprisingly, none of them could do it. So, good ol' Nebuchadnezzar, decreed that *all* his advisors, not just the ones who failed to interpret the dream, should be put to death.

Among the advisors on the hit list were Shadrach, Meshach, Abednego, and Daniel. When Daniel heard of the kill order he went to the king and interpreted the dream. All the advisors were saved and Daniel and his friends were promoted. The other advisors, the ones who would rat Shadrach, Meshach, and Abednego out later on, were not impressed that these foreigners were being promoted faster and higher than they were. They couldn't interpret dreams, but boy, were they good at holding a grudge.

Here's the other little tidbit you need to know, Nebuchadnezzar's dream was about a giant statue. That's right, a giant statue of a man with a head of gold, a chest of silver, a belly and thighs of bronze, legs of iron, and feet of iron and baked clay. The gold head represented Nebuchadnezzar 's kingdom, all the other parts represented the lesser kingdoms that would follow Babylon.

Low and behold, not long after his dream, ol' Nebuchadnezzar started construction of – you guessed it – a giant statue in the form of a man. Most speculate that it bore his own face, but more importantly it was gold from top to bottom. You see what's happening here right? The king was trying to change the future. Whether it was defiance or desperation, Nebuchadnezzar was making a clear and obvious statement: My kingdom *will not* end or diminish!

Nebuchadnezzar's statue was big – ridiculously big. It is recorded as being 90 feet tall. Next time you're out walking around, look for an apartment block or office building that is nine stories tall. Go stand next to the building and look up, waaaay up. That's where Shadrach, Meshach, and Abednego were standing.

Nebuchadnezzar's statue was built to intimidate, plain and simple. He wanted everyone standing in front of this thing to feel small, tiny, and powerless. He wanted the people to sense that, if it wanted to, the statue could literally take a step and squash them like bugs. The statue was built to carry a very clear and personal message from the king to his people.

There is a clay tablet known as the Babylonian Chronical housed in the British Museum. The cuneiform writing on the tablet records the history of the Babylonian Empire between the years 605 - 594 BCE. It tells us that, in 594 BCE, a revolt broke out in Babylon. Things got so bad there was even hand to hand combat inside the palace. Nebuchadnezzar, himself killed several insurgents with his own sword.

Most estimates put the events of Daniel chapter three right around this time. It is suspected that this statue christening on the plains of Dura was meant to serve a very intentional purpose.

- It was to remind everyone of their place
- It was to let everyone know exactly where they stood
- It was to make sure everyone knew exactly who was in charge
- If the king said jump, you said how high
- If the king said bow, you said how low

The last thing Nebuchadnezzar could afford to have happen here, on this day, was for anyone – especially three of his top officials – to challenge *his* authority.

I think that's why Nebuchadnezzar gave Shadrach, Meshach, and Abednego a couple chances to change their minds. It's possible he may have kind of liked these guys a bit, but more importantly, it would look better if they conformed. That's also why, when they refused, Nebuchadnezzar knew he had to make an extreme example of them.

The furnace Shadrach, Meshach, and Abednego were thrown into was most likely an iron ore smelter, a brick kiln, or a crematorium. Each of these had to reach between 1,000 and 1,300 degrees Celsius to successfully complete their tasks. I think it is safe to say the furnace wasn't at its max temp when Nebuchadnezzar instructed the men to stoke the fire seven times hotter because 7000 degrees Celsius is just tad hotter than the surface of the sun. However, it seems painfully clear that the furnace was blazing hot, because even the guards who threw Shadrach, Meshach and Abednego in were killed by the heat and flames.

But despite all the intimidation and threats, despite being bound by Nebuchadnezzar's strongest soldiers, despite feeling the heat of this raging inferno, even from yards away, when Shadrach, Meshach, and Abednego were given one final chance, their response is:

> *Shadrach, Meshach, and Abednego replied to the king, "O Nebuchadnezzar, we do not need to defend ourselves*

> *before you in this matter. If we are thrown into the blazing furnace, the God we serve is able to save us from it, and he will rescue us from your hand, O king. But even if he does not, we want you to know, O king, that we will not serve your gods or worship the image of gold you have set up." (Daniel 3:16-18 NIV)*

Shadrach, Meshach, and Abednego stare the maniacal, narcissistic and power-hungry king right in the eye and declare: no matter how tall your statue is, no matter how much you threaten us, no matter how tight our bonds are, no matter how hot you stoke that furnace, we still choose God over you. We still worship God, not you. We still follow God's plan, not yours.

Imagine you and I were to go skydiving together. This will never happen, at least not of my own volition, but go ahead and imagine it anyway. Once the plane has climbed to an appropriately terrifying height, we prepare to make our jump. Seconds before I leap out of the plane you ask me if I am confident that my parachute will open and adequately slow my plummeting towards earth. I look at you and smile with a confidence I can't even fathom mustering and say, "I am totally sure the parachute will work...but even if it doesn't, I'm jumping anyway!"

Shadrach, Meshach, and Abednego are so confident God will save them somehow. They are so certain about it they are willing to literally stake their lives on it. In the Sunday School version of this story, I always assumed that somehow they knew. Somehow they had received a heavenly text or a divine memo that assured them it was all going to work out okay. It definitely makes an awesome ending to the story that God actually does step in and save them!

However, my childhood assumptions are almost certainly incorrect. Shadrach, Meshach, and Abednego walked into the fire hoping, trusting, believing, but *not knowing* God would rescue them. Nonetheless, they boldly told Nebuchadnezzar that, even if God didn't step in, they were ready to trust the LORD and follow His design for their lives.

That amazes me! It's one thing to have a strong enough faith to look at a lousy situation and confidently declare, "God can fix this. God can make this right." But it's another thing altogether to look at a lousy situation and say, "Even if God doesn't fix this, I'm still trusting Him. I'm still relying on Him. I'm still living according to His design. I'm still following His path even if it leads me right into that fire."

You see, I don't read the story of Shadrach, Meshach, and Abednego because I need proof that God always fixes things because that doesn't always happen in this world. I don't read this story because I totally identify with Shadrach,

Meshach and Abednego and their unwavering faith in the face of unimaginable danger and fear. I read this story to be inspired to live a little more like that today, and tomorrow and the next day. I read this story to be reminded that it can be done and that living life God's way is worth the risks. Most importantly I read this story to be assured by the fact that when Shadrach, Meshach, and Abednego were thrown into the fire, when their trial was at its worst, God was right there in the flames with them.

> *But now, this is what the LORD says-- he who created you, O Jacob, he who formed you, O Israel: "Fear not, for I have redeemed you; I have summoned you by name; you are mine. When you pass through the waters, I will be with you; and when you pass through the rivers, they will not sweep over you. When you walk through the fire, you will not be burned; the flames will not set you ablaze. For I am the LORD, your God, the Holy One of Israel, your Savior; (Isaiah 43:1-3a NIV)*

HELLO
MY NAME IS
Daniel

In the Jungle, the Mighty Jungle

Hello, my name is Belteshazzar, but you can call me Daniel. My buddies, Shadrach, Meshach, Abednego and I were among the thousands of Israelites exiled from our homeland when the Babylonians conquered our nation. The Babylonian king, Nebuchadnezzar, educated us and trained us to be his administrators and advisors. God was with us and He blessed us, so we quickly advanced up the ladder of Babylonian government. That didn't sit very well with the locals.

Nonetheless, we continued to serve God and do our jobs faithfully. The more we succeeded, the more we were promoted. The more we were promoted, the more our Babylonian peers resented us. This went on for sixty-six years as I served the Babylonian kings.

One night, King Belshazzar was having a big party, essentially to celebrate how great he thought he was. I was not invited, which, to be honest, was fine by me. In the middle of the festivities a hand materialized out of thin air and wrote a message on the wall. No one could decipher the message and the king was beside himself. He turned white as a sheet and looked like he was about to pass out. Finally, someone remembered that I had interpreted the dreams of some of the previous kings, so I was called in.

I told the king, “I can interpret the message, but you are not going to like it. The message says: God has numbered the days of your reign. You have been weighed and found wanting. Your kingdom will be given over to the Persians.” That very night Darius the Mede invaded and Babylon fell to the Persian Empire.

The new king decided to appoint one hundred and twenty governors over the different regions of the country. He selected three of these men to be in charge of all the other governors. As it turned out, I was one of the three he chose, which did not sit well with my co-workers, but that was nothing new.

To make matters worse, things were about to get better. God blessed my work so much that the king was on the verge of appointing me ruler of the entire land of Babylon. You think that sounds awesome. My contemporaries did not. They were livid, so they embarked on a smear campaign. They wouldn’t be the first or last politicians to try and handle their problems this way. They thought if they could dig up enough dirt on me they could get me fired or at the very least make the king think twice about selecting me to run the country.

The only problem was they couldn't find any dirt. No skeletons in the closet. Nothing swept under the rug. I was squeaky clean and this infuriated them. They all got together in a back room somewhere to compare notes. They unanimously agreed the only way they would ever have something to hold over me was if they made it up themselves. So that's what they did.

A group of them went in and started buttering up the king. I mean they complimented him until his head was swimming in his own magnificence. Then, right at the climax of the flattery-palooza, one of them *spontaneously* suggested, "King, you're so awesome. We should make a law that no one can worship or pray to anyone but you, all month long – that's how awesome you are! Don't you guys agree?"

"Yeah, totally."

"Absolutely."

"Best. Law. Ever."

The king bought it, hook, line, and sinker. "Write it up boys, and I'll sign it into law," he declared. So, they did. If any man prays to anyone other than the great King Darius, he will be thrown into a den of lions.

When I heard the news, I was distraught. I prayed to God all the time and that's not something I was willing to give up. Of course, they all knew it too. So, I did what I always do when I find myself in a tight jam – I talked to God about it. I went out on my balcony, knelt down, and prayed.

Within minutes a large group of men burst through my door. They arrived so quickly it was obvious someone must have been watching my home, just waiting for me to pray. The men grabbed me and dragged me off to the palace. They held me outside the door for a moment as one man went in to verify that the king had officially signed the law and the ink was dry. Then they brought me in and said, "Daniel has broken the law. You know what you have to do."

The king didn't like it; in fact, he looked as hard as he could for a loophole, but there was none to be found. He had no legal choice but to throw me into the lion's den. They covered the opening with a large stone and sealed it, not just with the king's signet ring, but also the rings of all his nobles. I guess the other governors didn't trust the king to actually leave me in there once they all left.

Close your eyes for a moment and just try to imagine this. There I was, tossed down into a pit. A stone covered the opening and it was lights out time for me – literally and figuratively. My eyes were a little shoddy to begin with but in the dark? Forget about it. Lions on the other hand, well, they've got eyes like cats.

I couldn't see a thing, but I could hear prowling, growling, lions licking their chops, hungry cats jockeying for position, fighting over who gets the first bite just in case there's not enough of me to go around. I just laid there on the ground, with my eyes squeezed shut. No, it didn't make any difference since it was already pitch black in there, but it made me feel better somehow. I waited for the first chomp to pierce my skin and crush my bones. For a while, it seemed like the suspense would kill me before the lions did.

I waited and waited and waited. Maybe they didn't see me, I thought. But then one lion sniffed at my head. Another nuzzled my ribs. A third lion licked at my legs. They knew I was there alright, they just weren't interested. I laid there for so long, waiting for the end to come, I eventually dozed off.

The next thing I knew, the stone was being moved away and daylight was streaming into the den from above. I looked around for the first time since I had landed and saw myself encircled by lions sprawled lazily out on the dirt floor.

"Daniel? Are you down there?" the king shouted as soon as the stone was moved out of the way. "I was so stressed I couldn't sleep a wink all night long. I came at first light in hopes that somehow you might be still clinging to life down there."

I looked up at the king, my eyes still adjusting to the bright light of dawn, and said, "Great king, God sent an angel and closed the mouths of the lions. Take a look, I don't even have a single scratch on me! God protected me because I have always been faithful to Him and have never done anything wrong against you."

Some men lowered a rope and pulled me up out of the den. The king was so ticked off at having been played, he had all the men who had set me up, and their families, thrown into the den as soon as I was out. I know some people say those lions were just old or not hungry which is how I managed to last the night, but, I tell you, those poor other folks who got thrown in that morning were devoured before they even reached the ground.

After that day, the king issued a decree to every part of his empire saying: “Everyone must revere the God of Daniel. For He is the living God and He endures forever.”

You know, my wife always told me I was a man with poor taste, I guess those lions agreed.

Please don’t be mad, ladies, but, I don’t like Jane Austen movies. It’s not because the books are better. I have no clue if that is true because I’ve never read any of her books. I don’t have anything in particular against Jane, it’s just that her stories just aren’t up my alley. My wife disagrees with me on this point. So, on occasion, my love for my wife overrules my apathy towards Ms. Austen, and I will joyfully suffer through one of the films. At regular intervals during the show, we have to pause so my wife can clarify which character is which, who they used to fancy, who they currently fancy and who they will end up marrying. Following these updates, at least for a few minutes, the movie is more interesting and the storyline makes more sense. Then I get them all mixed up again.

I feel that way when I look at the story of Daniel. Sometimes I forget, or at the very least, overlook who some of the main characters really are. Once I'm reminded of who's who in the zoo, as my father would say, the story becomes much richer. So, just on the off chance that you're like me, let's recap exactly who we are talking about.

THE LIONS

The wow-factor of this story largely rests on our feline friends. Some skeptics suggest the lions were old and scrawny and therefore didn't pose any real threat to Daniel. Others hypothesize that some of Daniel's friends snuck in and fed them before he was dropped into the den.

In reality, the lions were there for one purpose. This was not a petting zoo. The lions were there to attack and kill, plain and simple. They would have been used either as a form of capital punishment, as in this case, for sport in gladiator-style competitions or to be hunted by the king. Either way, they were not weak, old or sickly.

Think about bull riding. The bulls in this sport are strong and powerful. They buck, jump, twist and turn. You would not go to a bull riding event at a rodeo and expect to see a cowboy riding old Bessy the milk cow!

Ancient documents tell us that in places where such lion's dens existed, people would throw small bits of food at the lions to get them riled up. Not enough to satisfy them, just enough to whet their appetites. Kind of like eating just one potato chip. Moreover, getting beaned in the head by tiny chunks of steak would leave the lions ready to devour anything that was thrown into the pit.

Even if the lions weren't hungry, they are territorial by nature and would have certainly mauled and gnawed on Daniel just for being on their turf. And yet the text says there wasn't a single scratch on him.

If any doubt remains about the lion's appetite all we have to do is watch, moments after Daniel is removed from the den. The king, who was angry that Daniel had been set up and that he had been tricked by his own advisors, had all the men who had conspired against Daniel and their families thrown into the same den with the same lions. The text says the lions leapt up and tore them apart before they hit the ground.

So be sure you properly appreciate the severity of the danger Daniel was facing. Being cast into the lion's den was not an idle threat; it was a guaranteed death sentence.

THE CONSPIRATORS

The second group of characters to understand in this story

are these guys called the satraps, advisors, Chaldeans or administrators – depending on your version.

Like Shadrach, Meshach, and Abednego, Daniel was among the young men taken from Israel, educated in Babylon and given government jobs. Of course, there were some of the native Babylonians, the Chaldeans, who weren't really happy with that plan, especially when these foreigners advanced higher and faster than they did.

In Daniel chapter two, King Nebuchadnezzar has a dream that he asks his advisors to interpret. They are unable to do so, and therefore the king orders that all of his advisors be killed off, even the ones that weren't in the room at the time. And among that hit list were Shadrach, Meshach, Abednego, and Daniel. To make a long story short, Daniel interprets the dream and all the advisors are spared the executioners ax. Then,

> *The king placed Daniel in a high position and lavished many gifts on him. He made him ruler over the entire province of Babylon and placed him in charge of all its wise men. Moreover, at Daniel's request the king appointed Shadrach, Meshach and Abednego administrators over the province of Babylon, while Daniel himself remained at the royal court. (Daniel 2:48-49 NIV)*

I know you think these administrators would have been thankful to Daniel for having saved their necks, but instead, they were just ticked off and jealous that these foreigners had been promoted over them and put in charge of them.

In Daniel chapter three we have the story of Shadrach, Meshach, and Abednego in the fiery furnace. If you're wondering who ratted the boys out when they didn't bow to Nebuchadnezzar's statue, here's a little hint:

> *At this time some astrologers (or Chaldeans) came forward and denounced the Jews. They said to King Nebuchadnezzar, "May the king live forever! Your Majesty has issued a decree that everyone who hears the sound of the horn, flute, zither, lyre, harp, pipe and all kinds of music must fall down and worship the image of gold, and that whoever does not fall down and worship will be thrown into a blazing furnace. But there are some Jews whom you have set over the affairs of the province of Babylon —Shadrach, Meshach and Abednego—who pay no attention to you, Your Majesty. They neither serve your gods nor worship the image of gold you have set up." (Daniel 3:8-12 NIV)*

Can you hear the animosity in their voice as they denounce the Jews? There are some *Jews* that *you* have set over the affairs of Babylon *(and over us too, thank you very much).* They *pay no attention* to you O king. They *don't serve* your god. They *won't worship* your image.

So, Shadrach, Meshach, and Abednego get thrown into the fiery furnace, but instead of being incinerated, they just walked out. When the smoke clears, they are unscorched, unsinged and unscented by the fire. And the story ends by saying this:

> *Then the king promoted Shadrach, Meshach, and Abednego in the province of Babylon. (Daniel 3: 30 NIV)*

You can imagine how that sat with those Babylonian administrators.

In chapter five we have the story of King Belshazzar who's having a self-celebratory party. And during the middle of the festivities, a disembodied floating hand appears and writes on the wall. Again, the king summons the enchanters, Chaldeans, and diviners to decipher the message. And just like Nebuchadnezzar's dream, none of them could do it. Eventually, someone suggests getting Daniel to take a look at it, so, since he apparently wasn't invited to the party, someone went to fetch him. Daniel decodes the message, and even though the message isn't particularly favorable to the king, the story ends with:

> *Then at Belshazzar's command, Daniel was clothed in purple, a gold chain was placed around his neck, and he was proclaimed third highest ruler in the kingdom. (Daniel 5:8-9 NIV)*

Does anyone see a pattern here? Over and over, the Babylonian advisors get an incredibly lousy performance review at work, immediately followed by Daniel and/or his friends getting honored with a big promotion!

There's one last straw we need to add to this camel's back. The same night Daniel told Belshazzar that the writing was on the wall, the Persians invaded and Darius became king in Babylon. And one of the first things Darius did was appoint 120 satraps. Most likely taking people from Belshazzar's government who already knew the country and how things ran. Which means this is essentially the same group of advisors that we've been tracking all along. Darius appoints three men as administrators over all of them and Daniel is one of the three. You may read that and think nothing has really changed. After all, Belshazzar had already made Daniel third highest in the land. You're absolutely right until this happens:

> *Now Daniel so distinguished himself among the administrators and the satraps by his exceptional qualities that the king planned to set him over the whole kingdom. At this, the administrators and the satraps tried to find grounds for charges against Daniel. (Daniel 6:3-4a NIV)*

Virtually his entire life Daniel has been dogged and hounded, by this same group of people. Maybe not always the exact same individuals, but as a collective group these Babylonian administrators have had it out for Daniel and his friends since day one. The more Daniel succeeded and advanced, the more these guys hated his guts. Every time he did what they couldn't. Every time he was rewarded, and they were not. They were more and more determined to take him down.

And finally, here in chapter six, they decide to do something about it. This is not a plan hatched on a whim. This is no petty squabble. These guys view Daniel as their arch nemesis who needs to be dealt with once and for all, with extreme prejudice.

Which brings us to our third, and most important character in this story.

DANIEL

To properly appreciate how long Daniel has been harassed by these guys, you have to realize how old Daniel was. Daniel and Shadrach, Meshach and Abednego were contemporaries and most scholars agree they were taken from Israel at more or less the same age. Since Shadrach, Meshach, and Abednego were around 20 at the time of the fiery furnace, we naturally assume that Daniel must have also been 20ish when he's tossed into the lion's den. Perhaps a little bit of time has passed, so let say mid to late 20s. Early 30s tops. And that sentiment is often endorsed by the pictures we see of Daniel in the lion's den. But that estimate is not exactly on the mark.

Here's a little bit of math for you. We know Jerusalem was first conquered by the Babylonians in 605 BCE. Daniel, along with Shadrach, Meshach, and Abednego, would have been taken into captivity at that time. The Persian Empire, led by Darius the Mede occupied Babylon in 539 BCE. That's sixty-six years later. Most estimates put Daniel at around fifteen years old at the time he was taken into captivity. Which means Daniel was approximately 81 years old at the time of this story. That's significant for a couple reasons.

First, when we see Daniel as a young guy, full of muscles, really strong, virile and energetic we think maybe, just maybe he might have had a little bit of a chance to fend off the lions, at least for a little while. The truth is, even a strapping young lad wouldn't stand a chance against a pride of man-eating lions, but we kind of have that image in our head. But we're not talking about a strong young man in the lion's den. We're talking about a senior citizen who is 81 years old! With all due respect to octogenarians everywhere, at 81 he was lucky to survive the fall, let alone fend off the lions.

But more significantly, we have to realize that Daniel has been challenged and harassed by these same guys for six decades. This isn't just a "they woke up on the wrong side of the bed, but they'll get over it" kind of thing. This isn't a they got their nose out of joint, but they'll get over it kind of thing. These guys have been carrying a grudge for a lifetime. It may have even been passed down from one generation to another.

And that is a lot of bitterness under the bridge, and these guys just couldn't seem to get over it.

So, for anyone who has ever had a grumpy neighbor next door, for anyone who works for a lousy manager or a crummy boss, for anyone who has to deal with a curmudgeonly co-worker, an irritating relative or even an ornery public official, this story is for you.

Unfortunately, Daniel's example doesn't tell us how to get rid of these persistent personal pests, but it does tell us the secret to being able to live with them. When Daniel found out about the King's new law, the first thing he did was go to his room to pray. In fact, the text says that it was his habit to pray like this three times every day, (and I'm pretty sure it's not referring to breakfast, lunch, dinner). Daniel took a significant chunk of time out of his day, every day, to pray. After following the plot of the first six chapters, I'm pretty confident that a lot of those daily prayers over the past sixty years had included the Chaldeans.

When the law was signed, Daniel's first instinct was to pray about it. I don't think he was praying specifically in defiance of the law, I think he prayed because that is the way he always dealt with tough situations. This law has come up and he knows he can't submit to it, so what should he do? Well, let's talk to God about it.

Now, before you write this chapter off as not practical, or something that doesn't work in the real world, consider what you're saying. If prayer really is what we say it is, and really does what we say it does, it would be preposterous for us to not be praying all the time about everything.

Do you remember the red phone that used to sit in Commissioner Gordon's office that was a direct line to Batman? What if I hooked you up with a direct line to the most powerful, wealthy, philanthropic person in the world, who just happens to be over the moon nuts about you? Why on earth wouldn't you make the call?

That's what God has offered you. He's on the other end, waiting, listening, eager to hear your voice. The question is, will we make the call?

> *Do not be anxious about anything, but in every situation, by prayer and petition, with thanksgiving, present your requests to God. And the peace of God, which transcends all understanding, will guard your hearts and your minds in Christ Jesus. (Philippians 4:6-7 NIV)*

HELLO
MY NAME IS
Esther

A Meal Fit for a King

Hello, my name is Hadassah. Hadassah was my Jewish name, but in my younger years it was advantageous to keep your country of origin discretely hidden, so to most people, I was known simply as Esther. You see, I was born in exile. My people had been captured by the Babylonians who were eventually overtaken by the Persians. Both my parents died when I was very young and so, I was an orphan, raised by my cousin Mordecai, in a foreign land. This is the story of how I became Queen of the Empire!

Before we go any further I need to set a few things straight. This is no Cinderella story. Disney will never make a film about my life, at least not an accurate one. You see, I became the queen of the great King Xerxes. The word great here refers to political and military prowess, not the quality of his character. Most of the time, Xerxes was a chauvinistic, drunken jerk.

I was not Xerxes' first queen. That title goes to a woman named Vashti. When I was just a teenager, minding my own business, living with cousin Mordi, King Xerxes threw a colossal party. Xerxes loved to party, but this was one for the ages. It was a six-month-long kegger for all his noblemen, with all the wine and food you could possibly want. Xerxes arranged for all the best art and jewelry and anything else in the kingdom that showed off his opulence to be continually paraded in front of all his inebriated friends.

But there was one thing of beauty that had not yet been put on display for the noblemen to gawk at – Queen Vashti. So, the King sent messengers to tell the queen to come display herself for the men to ogle, wearing her crown, a smile, and not much else. The queen declined the request, so the king sent men back to order her to appear. She refused.

"You can't let her get away with this!" all the noblemen at the party protested. "If word gets out that the queen has refused the command of the king, *all* our wives will suddenly start refusing to do everything we tell them to. And we can't have that."

So, King Xerxes stripped (ironically) Vashti of her crown and title and banished her. However, a king can't be without a queen, regardless of how big his harem is, so a search was conducted for a suitable replacement. The king dispatched men across his kingdom to find the most beautiful young women they could. When they found a woman, they thought might be suitable, they would take her to the palace. Not invite her, take her. I was one of the many women taken from my home and brought to the palace.

We spent an entire year in the palace, being trained, tanned, primped, plucked, styled, dressed and made up. At the end of that year, the king began test driving each one of us. Each night one of us would be randomly called to his chambers and given our chance to *impress* him. Needless to say, intellect and conversational skills weren't at the top of the list of qualifications he was interested in. He was looking for someone to be arm candy at public functions and please him whenever he was feeling frisky but wasn't in the mood for one of his regular harem girls.

I lost this competition and therefore, as his chosen favorite, was selected to become the new queen.

All this time, my cousin Mordi would hang around outside the palace every single day, keeping an eye on the windows, hoping to catch a glimpse of me so he could see that I was alright. On one of these days, he heard some men conspiring to assassinate the king. He got word of the plot to me and I warned the king. The plan was thwarted and the king survived, which, to be honest, I had mixed feelings about.

King Xerxes' right-hand man was a real low life named Haman. Haman was almost as narcissistic and arrogant as the king; perhaps that's why they got along so well. When Haman would walk out of the palace, he expected everyone to bow and everyone did, well, almost everyone. Cousin Mordi refused to bow which infuriated Haman. I remember as a young girl, Mordi would tell me a story of these three young Jews in Babylon who refused to bow to anyone but the LORD. Perhaps, you've heard that story too. I think this was his own way of living out that principle.

Haman was so enraged, he went to the king and said, "There is a group of people who are not assimilating well into the empire. They do not follow our customs or keep our laws. We need to get rid of them. Every last one of them."

"What do you suggest?" the king asked.

"Let's designate one specific day. And on that day, anyone who wants to, can kill a Jew and seize his property. That way, every man, woman, and child from this contentious people will be eradicated."

The king liked the sound of Haman's plan, so they picked dates out of a hat and decided that on the 13th day of the 12th month it would be open season on all Jews. An edict bearing the king's signet was sent across the empire from Palestine to India.

When the Jews heard of this proclamation, they dressed in rags, refused to eat and fell into deep mourning. I knew nothing about it at the time because I was locked up in the palace. But Mordi slipped a message to me and explained what was happening. Then he told me that I had to go to the king and change his mind.

I tried to explain to him that I could no more go to the king without being summoned than Vashti could refuse to go to him when called. Besides it had been a whole month since the king had last asked for me for any reason, and for all I knew he was tired of my company and had directed his affections to someone newer and younger. But Mordi told me God was going to use my position in the palace to save His people.

I mustered up all the courage I could manage and went to the throne room. When I entered, the king extended his golden scepter to me which meant my life had been spared, at least for the moment. The king asked me what I wanted.

"Your majesty," I replied. "I would like you and Haman to come to a banquet tonight."

The king agreed and later that night I hosted Xerxes and Haman at a luxurious feast. They ate, drank and were very merry. However, the king knew I had risked my life for something more than a dinner invitation, so he asked me again what it was I really wanted."

"Grant me just a little more time, great king," I said. "If both you and Haman will come back tomorrow I will prepare another feast for you and then I will present my request."

The king agreed and Haman went home on cloud nine because he had been invited to two such exclusive engagements. That night the king was troubled and could not sleep. He asked one of his servants to read the record of the events of his reign. When the servant recounted the assassination plot foiled by Mordecai's intervention, the king asked if Mordecai had been rewarded for his actions – at this time he didn't know that Mordi was my cousin. The servant said no reward or honor had been given.

The next day the king asked Haman what should be done to honor a very great man. Haman, egotistical man that he was, assumed this great honor was going to be bestowed on him, so he held nothing back.

"You should bring out one of the king's robes and a horse that the king himself has ridden. Put the robe on the man and the man on the horse. Have them led through the entire town for everyone to see. And as they go along, have the man who is leading the horse shout out, 'This is a man the king honors!'"

The king took Haman's advice and did just as he had suggested for Mordecai. Haman was livid. He immediately went home and erected a 75-foot-tall gallows which he planned to hang cousin Mordi on the first chance he got.

That evening the king and Haman came, once more, to the banquet I had prepared for them. Towards the end of the meal, the king asked me again, why I had invited them.

"Ask for anything," the king declared. "And it's yours. Even if you ask for half of my kingdom, you've got it. Now tell me, what is it you really want from me?"

"Oh great king," I began, even more nervous than I thought I would be, which is really saying something. "I want you to spare my life. A death sentence has been pronounced on me. And not just me, but all of my family and relatives. In truth, there is a price on the head of every last one of my countrymen."

The king flew into a rage, which was not an uncommon thing. "Who would dare conspire to do such a thing to *my* queen?" he demanded.

"It was Haman," I answered. "He has plotted to kill all of the people of Israel, of which I am one."

Haman was slinking under the table and eyeing the exits just in case, but the king beat him to it. Xerxes stormed out of the room. Through the window, I could see him pacing frantically in the garden. Meanwhile, inside Haman knew that his proverbial goose was cooked. In a last-ditch effort to save his own skin, Haman fell to the ground and flopped himself upon the couch where I was sitting.

Right about then, Xerxes returned to the room. Haman was still pleading with me for mercy, but that's not what it looked like from where the king stood.

"Traitor!" the king exclaimed. "Not only would you plot to murder my queen, but now you are trying to take advantage of her in my very own palace?"

The king gave orders that Haman should be hung on the gallows he constructed himself to kill Mordecai on. Then he called my cousin and me into the throne room.

"The traditions of our land make it impossible to repeal the law Haman created and had me sign. However, what I can do is let you write a new law of your own, whatever you want, to protect your people, and I will sign it."

Cousin Mordi wrote a law stating that for one day, all the Jews in the empire would be permitted to assemble together and defend themselves by whatever means necessary without any repercussions. Naturally, the date he selected for this to occur was the 13th day of the 12th month. The king signed the new law and sent it to every corner of the empire.

When the fateful day came, there were thousands, including Haman's sons, who attempted to take advantage of the original law and attacked the Jews, hoping to seize their property. However, all the Jews worked together and fought back. There were also many other city officials and government representatives who fought alongside the people of Israel because Mordecai's reputation had spread across the empire and the people knew he had great influence with the king.

The following day, all the Jews across the land, observed a day of rest and celebration. It became an annual feast that continues right up to this very day.

I was recently at a wedding. It was nice. Pretty decorations, fancy dresses, and sappy music. The reception had good food, sentimental speeches and, of course, a slide show retrospective of the lives of the happy couple. All in all a lovely day. I grew up thinking Esther's story was kind of like that. Peasant girl marries the king. Orphan girl becomes queen. It sounds romantic. It was not. And that perspective colored my understanding of the critical moment of this story.

Occasionally, someone will come into my office while I'm right in the middle of writing down, or typing up a thought, at which point I have two choices: 1) ignore them momentarily, or 2) pause what I am writing, talk to the visitor and then, hang on, what was I saying again? Nonetheless, when I experience one of those untimely interruptions, at worst I'm a little frustrated, but typically not enough to inhibit my ability to be polite.

That's how I viewed Esther's choice to go talk to the king. I assumed that her situation was like mine. Sometimes my wife interrupts the football game to remind me the garbage still has not been taken to the curb. Sure, that irritates me, mostly because I don't want to have to take the garbage to the curb, but I can honestly say I've never felt the urge to execute her for it.

That's how I always read this story. Yeah, yeah, I get it, the law states that no one can enter the king's presence without being summoned and if you do you could end up with your head on the chopping block. But, c'mon. This is his queen, his wife. Presumably, at some point, the mother of his children. Technically that might be what the law says, but seriously, was it *really* that big of a risk?

Yes, yes it was. Xerxes is an ill-tempered impulsive man who did not put up with anyone challenging his authority in even the slightest of ways. Theirs is not a love story. It is not even an arranged marriage. She is there only because Xerxes liked the way she looked and the way she, ahem, did other things. She is property to him and he displays time and again that he has no qualms about getting rid of people who don't cater to his whims.

Esther's willingness to do what God asked to protect God's people is nothing short of heroic. Don't let anyone ever tell you otherwise.

Of course, this enriched reading of the text presents us with a problem too. In the fairy-tale version of this story, we all stand up and cheer when Mordecai speaks his famous line:

> *"Who knows if perhaps you were made queen for just such a time as this?" (Esther 4:14b NIV)*

Yeah! God did all this great stuff and made you queen! And as if that's not enough, He did it all so you would be in the right place at the right time with enough power to save His people. Yeah, God!

But that's not how the story goes, is it? No, Esther's rise to queen was not a luxurious season starring on The Bachelorette. It was an unjust and exploitive series of events. If someone did today what Xerxes did to Esther they would be charged with human trafficking and statutory rape. How can we possibly suggest that God put her through all of that just so He could use her to counteract Haman's law? If that's the way God works, I want nothing to do with Him.

I cannot say this strongly enough: *God does not work like that.* God *can't* work like that because it is totally contradictory to the very nature of who He is. God *does not* cause bad things to happen. Not then, not now, not ever.

I have seen far too many people turn their backs on God because they were experiencing some terrible, sometimes traumatic, event in their life when some well-meaning person suggested that their current heartache was just God's way of accomplishing something good somewhere down the line.

Please hear me, now: *God doesn't do that.* God hates, with a holy passion, anything that hurts people. Anything that damages individuals. Anything that destroys His most beloved creation. Yes, God will work in whatever messed up and miserable situation He finds people in to try to build something good and worthwhile out of the rubble. *That is what God does.* Don't let anyone, ever, convince you that any of your wounds and scars exist because God wanted it that way.

What Mordecai is saying to his cousin Esther is not, "Maybe God put you through all that horrifically painful stuff, just so He could get access to the throne room." If God wanted to find a way to get a message to the king, He could have found a way. For crying out loud, in the previous chapter we saw a disembodied hand appear out of nowhere and write on the wall!

If God wanted to get through to Xerxes, He could have done it without Esther. Mordecai says as much himself when he tells Esther, if you don't do it, God will find another way, (Esther 4:14). But God loves bringing something good out of a bad situation. He loves building something new out of the broken. He loves nurturing life amid the toxic. He loves extracting value from the pointless. He loves to redeem His people from the corruption of this world.

Paul writes,

> *And we know that in all things God works for the good of those who love him, who have been called according to his purpose. (Romans 8:28 NIV)*

In all things – the good, the bad and the ugly – God works to make something good come out of it. If you ever wonder what God is up to, here is the answer: He is working for the good. In fact, according to James, the brother of Jesus, every good thing comes from God. *(James 1:17)*. If you've experienced it, and it was good, James says you have the working of God to thank for it.

Unfortunately, God is not the only power at work in our world. There are spiritual forces of evil that work to destroy everything good God has created. There are also, the forces of nature which lack malicious intent but can still inflict damage. And, of course, we are all dramatically influenced by the effects of human nature – both our own and in the lives of people around us. We can see all three of these forces inflicting pain and hardship in the story of Esther. You have likely seen their handiwork up close in your own life.

Whatever trials or heartache you have faced, always remember they exist in spite of God's working, not because of it. And whatever good things you have been blessed with, whether it be experiences, possessions or relationships, know that they are simply a foretaste of the good He would like to fill your life with. In this world we may never experience the full measure of good He desires for us, but God won't ever stop trying.

Hello, My Name is Esther

Epilogue

As I pen the final pages of this book it occurs to me that you, the reader, may be left with a few questions – two in particular.

The first question I suspect some of you are asking is, "What about the story of ________?" There are, without a doubt, dozens and dozens of other great stories in the Bible. Unfortunately, space did not allow me to delve into the stories of Adam & Eve, Cain & Able, Noah, Abraham, Isaac, Jacob, Joseph, Hannah, Samuel, Nehemiah, Job, and many others in this particular volume. Perhaps, someday I will have the opportunity to tell their stories as well. Some of the stories that were omitted this time around, particularly those out of the book of Genesis, were passed over this time because I already recounted them to a large degree in my 2016 publication: *The Book: The Story of God and Humanity.* To cover some of those same stories again here would have been somewhat redundant. Other stories were not included simply because space was limited and choices had to be made.

The second question that might be rattling around in your mind is, "Did all of this stuff actually happen the way you say it happened?" Well, yes, and not exactly. I have done my utmost to investigate the scriptures to ensure that the facts of the stories, as the Bible details them, are faithfully recounted in these pages. I have also taken a measure of artistic license to fill in some of the gaps and flesh things out. In other words, the Biblical facts of the story are unchanged, but the supplemental dialogue and descriptions have been added to create a greater sense of connection between the reader and these stories' characters. These embellishments are not meant to be taken as verified scripture but are merely offered as a way to get a sense of having been there. For those interested in reading the pure Biblical account, a list of where to find the primary text of each of the stories in this book are provided below:

Moses & Pharaoh – *Exodus 1-15*
Joshua & Jericho – *Joshua 1-6*
Balaam – *Numbers 22-24*
Gideon – *Judges 6-8*
Deborah & Barak – *Judges 4-5*
Samson – *Judges 13-16*
Ruth – *Ruth 1-4*
David & Goliath – *1 Samuel 17*
Jonah – *Jonah 1-4*
Elijah on Mount Carmel – *1 Kings 18*
Naboth – *1 Kings 21*
Elisha – *1 Kings 19, 2 Kings 2-13*
Shadrach, Meshach & Abednego – *Daniel 1-3*
Daniel & the Lion's Den - *Daniel 5-6*
Esther – *Esther 1-10*

Other titles from Shekinah Reflections you might enjoy:

It can be a daunting task to pick up a copy of the Bible and make any sense of it. It's a very long book. It has sections that can seem downright dull and others so complex that the best scholars still puzzle over them. THE BOOK retells the powerful story of God and people in a way that both first-time readers and experienced students of the Bible can relate. In his humorous but authentic style, Parker has captured the storyline of the Bible and pieced it together in a way that will connect with today's reader. Real life examples from his own experiences will make you chuckle, but also serve to bring clarity and meaning to the story.

The unmistakable thread, that runs from cover to cover of the Bible, is God's passionate pursuit of all humanity. This is the God who never gives up. This is the God who loves even those who spit in his face and curse his name. In the pages of THE BOOK, Parker paints a vivid mosaic of the character of the God who longs for a personal relationship with every individual. It's not about knowledge or performance, it's about the Creator who literally pulls out all the stops to proclaim to His creation, "Please come home where you will be loved unconditionally." In the brokenness of our world today, that is a message we all need to hear.

Parker's words successfully balance dramatic storytelling and engaging scripture in an authentic way. THE BOOK will seize your attention and point you toward the greatest story ever told.

Other titles from Shekinah Reflections you might enjoy:

It's more than a job. It's calling. So why are so many pastors in North America suffering from burn out, depression, anxiety or even suicidal thoughts?

Holy Toast offers a glimpse inside the everyday life of a minister. And not just a quick look at the day-to-day landscape, but also the deep emotional valleys of what is often a lonely, misunderstood profession.

Parker's years in ministry have given him insight into keeping ministers from burning out while doing the thing they love to do – serving in God's Kingdom. Calling upon those years of experience and the perspective he gleaned from observing his father's decades in ministry, Parker creates a roadmap to not only keep ministers in the pulpit but helping them from burning out while there. The book offers tips to help keep pastors from hitting the wall emotionally speaking.

Shekinah
Reflections
PUBLICATIONS

Made in the USA
Middletown, DE
30 May 2018